S.No.		Chapter Name	Page No.
		CONTENTS	1-3
1.		**DATABASE MANAGEMENT SYSTEM FUNDAMENTALS**	4
	1.1	Introduction	4
	1.2	DBMS Concepts	5
	1.3	Types of Database Users	14
	1.4	Evolution of Database Management Systems (DBMSs)	16
	1.5	Disadvantages or Problems with Conventional File Oriented or Processing Systems	17
	1.6	Advantages of Database Management Systems (DBMS)	19
	1.7	DBMS Additional Advantages	21
	1.8	DBMS Disadvantages	21
	1.9	Major Components in a Database System Environment	22
	1.10	Architecture or Structure of DBMS or Major components of DBMS	24
	1.11	Database Development using Three Schema Architecture	27
	1.12	Data Independence	28
	1.13	Self Assessment Questions	29
2.		**DATABASE MODELS**	30
	2.1	Introduction	30
	2.2	Definition of Data Model	31
	2.3	Database Models	31
	2.4	Types or Categories of Database Models	32
	2.5	Data Modeling	40
	2.6	Self Assessment Questions	42
3.		**DATABASE ENVIRONMENT**	43
	3.1	Database Systems in the Organization	43
	3.2	Strategic Database Planning	47
	3.3	Database and Management Control	53
	3.4	The Information Domain	55
	3.5	Risks and Costs of Database Management Systems (DBMSs)	60
	3.6	Self Assessment Questions	61
4.		**DATABASE DEVELOPMENT**	62
	4.1	Introduction	62
	4.2	Database Development under the Control of the Information Systems	62

	4.3	Database Development	66
	4.4	Classification of Database Management Systems	70
	4.5	Core database Technology Trend	71
	4.6	When is DBMS Inappropriate?	71
	4.7	The main characteristics of the database approach	72
	4.8	The goals of a Database Management System	72
	4.9	Self Assessment Questions	73
5.	**DATABASE DESIGN**		74
	5.1	Introduction	74
	5.2	Database Design	74
	5.3	Data Modeling / Database Design	74
	5.4	Steps in Database Design	75
	5.5	Self assessment questions	80
6.	**CONCEPTUAL DATABASE DESIGN**		81
	6.1	Introduction	81
	6.2	Principles of Conceptual Database Design	81
	6.3	Advantages of Conceptual Database Models	82
	6.4	Conceptual Data Models	83
	6.5	Aggregation	88
	6.6	Entity-Relationship (ER) data model and Entity-Relationship Diagrams (ERDs)	89
	6.7	Modeling Conceptual Objects versus Physical Objects	99
	6.8	Entity Relationship Diagram (ERD) Example	100
	6.9	Self Assessment Questions	101
7.	**RELATIONAL DATA MODEL AND NORMALIZATION**		102
	7.1	Introduction	102
	7.2	Relational Data Model (RDM)	102
	7.3	Relational Keys	105
	7.4	Integrity Constraints	107
	7.5	Converting Entity Relationship Diagrams (ERDs) Into Relations	108
	7.6	Functional Dependencies (FDs)	115
	7.7	Normalization	115
	7.8	Self assessment questions	125
8.	**RELATIONAL ALGEBRA AND RELATIONAL CALCULUS**		126
	8.1	Relational Algebra	126
	8.2	Relational Algebric Operations	127

	8.3	Relational Calculus	129
	8.4	Relational Calculus Operations	130
	8.5	Self assessment questions	131
9.	**SQL SCHEMA AND SQL OBJECTS**		132
	9.1	Schema	132
	9.2	Database Schema	132
	9.3	Database Instance	133
	9.4	DDL Statements	133
	9.5	Database Languages	138
	9.6	Views	139
10.	**DATA MANIPULATION**		148
	10.1	Data Manipulation Language (DML) Statements	148
	10.2	INSERT Statement	149
	10.3	UPDATE Statement	149
	10.4	DELETE Statement	150
	10.5	SELECT Statement	150
	10.6	JOINS	151
	10.7	Query Languages	155
	10.8	Graphical Query Language	155
	10.9	Self Assessment Questions	164
	REFERENCES		165-167

CHAPTER 1

DATABASE MANAGEMENT SYSTEM FUNDAMENTALS

Objectives

- ✓ To know the meaning of data, Information, Database, DBMS, RDBMS
- ✓ To study the features of File processing system and Database System
- ✓ To learn Advantages and Disadvantages of DBMS
- ✓ To understand the need of database
- ✓ To understand Database Application, Data Dictionary
- ✓ To study Components of DBMS Environment
- ✓ To understand Components of DBMS
- ✓ To know about responsibilities of Database Users
- ✓ To understand Three Schema database Architecture
- ✓ To understand Data Independence

Chapter Structure

1.1 Introduction

1.2 DBMS Concepts

1.3 Types of Database Users

1.4 Evolution of Database Management Systems (DBMSs)

1.5 Disadvantages or Problems with Conventional File Oriented or Processing Systems

1.6 Advantages of Database Management Systems (DBMS)

1.7 DBMS Additional Advantages

1.8 DBMS Disadvantages

1.9 Major Components in a Database System Environment

1.10 Architecture or Structure of DBMS or Major components of DBMS

1.11 Database Development using Three Schema Architecture

1.12 Data Independence

1.13 Self Assessment Questions

1.1 Introduction

An organization must have accurate, timely, relevant, and reliable data for efficient and effective decision making. Data management is easy when data is small. When data is large data management is very difficult. A database is a collection of interrelated data of a particular organization. Computer databases are mandatory for efficient and effective management of large data. A database is a shared, integrated computer structure that stores different types of data details.

Database management system (DBMS) is a complex software system that manages and controls the data stored in the database effectively. DBMS enables the data in the database to be shared among multiple applications or users. DBMS allows for efficient and effective management of large databases. A DBMS supports many different types of databases. It works as an interface between the user and the database. It manages and controls the interaction between the end user and the database. The primary goal of a DBMS is to store and retrieve data in the database efficiently, effectively, and conveniently in a controlled manner.

There exist many relational database management systems (RDBMSs) software packages in the market from different vendors. Important RDBMSs are – Oracle, M.S. SQL Server, DB2, MYSQL, Sybase, Informix, Ingress, Teradata, M.S. Access,

1.2 DBMS Concepts

Datum - Any single value is called datum. Data is plural of datum.

1.2.1 Data

Data is defined in many ways:

1. Data are facts or values used for creating information, which is used for decision making.
2. Data means meaningful facts, raw values, collection of ideas, text, graphics, images, sound, video segments.
3. Known values or facts that can be recorded and have an implicit meaning.
4. Data are raw facts. The word raw indicates that the facts have not yet been processed.
5. Data and information are interchangeable

Data is defined as collection of raw facts. Data are processed through models to create information. Data can exists in a variety of forms – numbers, text, bits and bytes, images, diagrams, charts, figures etc.

Data is defined as a body of facts or figures, which have been gathered systematically for one or more specific purposes. The data are collected and used for problem solving and decision making. Data is required for the operation of any organization. Data constitute the building blocks of information. Many people use the terms "data" and "information" as synonyms but these two terms actually convey very distinct concepts

Data is a collection of facts or values such as student names, marks, classes, addresses, ages, courses, qualification etc. In computer science data is defined as stored details of objects such as universities, colleges, students, hostels, accounts, doctors, actors, movies, books, marks, exams, subjects, companies, games, etc and events. Examples for data are – student grades, marks, hall ticket numbers, telephone numbers, telephone bills, and addresses.

Data can exist in the forms of

- Linguistic expressions (e.g. name, age, address, date, ownership)
- Symbolic expressions (e.g. traffic signs)
- Mathematical expressions (e.g. $b^2 = 4ac$, $y = mx + c$, $E = mc^2$)
- Signals (e.g. electromagnetic waves)

1.2.2 Information

Processed or refined or summarized data is called information. Organized or arranged or meaningful or useful or convenient data is called information. Information consists of data, images, text, documents, voice, bits, bytes, numbers, text, diagrams, charts, figures etc.

Information is the back bone of any organization. Accurate, timely and relevant information details are the key element to good decision making. Good decision making is the key for the survival of any organization in the competitive global business environment. For example, marks in computer science exam of third year B.Com students of Sri Venkateswara arts and science college are given below:

90, 60, 55, 85, 95, 45, 70, 65, 50, 75, 80, 99   …. Data

45, 50, 55, 60, 65, 70, 75, 80, 85, 90, 95, 99   …. Information (increase order)

99, 95, 90, 85, 80, 75, 70, 65, 60, 55, 50, 45   …. Information (decrease order)

Maximum marks = 99, minimum marks = 45   …. Information

Average, second maximum, second minimum, third maximum, third minimum, n^{th} maximum, n^{th} minimum are information details.

1. Good decisions require good information derived from raw facts.

2. Information is defined as data which have been processed into a form that is meaningful to a recipient and is of perceived value in current or prospective decision making.

3. Although data are ingredients of information, not all data make useful information.

4. Data that is not properly collected and organized are a burden rather than an asset to an information user

5. Data that make useful information for one person may not be useful to another person.

6. Information is only useful to its recipients when it is
   - relevant (to its intended purposes and with appropriate level of required detail)
   - reliable, accurate and verifiable (by independent means)
   - up-to-date and timely (depending on purposes)
   - complete (in terms of attribute, spatial and temporal coverage)
   - intelligible (i.e. comprehensible by its recipients)
   - consistent (with other sources of information)
   - convenient/easy to handle and adequately protected

7. the function of an information system is to change "data" into "information", using the following processes :
   a. conversion – transforming data from one format to another, from one unit of measurement to another, and/or from one feature classification to another
   b. organization – organizing or re-organizing data according to database management rules and procedures so that they can be accessed cost-effectively
   c. structuring – formatting or re-formatting data so that they can be acceptable to a particular software application or information system
   d. modeling – including statistical analysis and visualization of data that will improve user's knowledge base and intelligence in decision making

8. The concepts of "organization" and "structure" are crucial to the functioning of information systems – without organization and structure it is simply impossible to turn data into information

1.2.3 Difference between data and information

Data	Information
1. Collection of facts or raw values	1. Processed data is called information
2. May or may not be useful for decision making	2. Useful for decision making
3. Example for data is 60, 40, 80, 100, 20	3. Example for information 20, 40, 60, 80, 100
4. Input of a computer is called data	4. Output of a computer is called information
5. Values taken as it is called data	5. Refined values are called information

Characteristics of quality information are–Accuracy, Timeliness, Relevancy, and Reliable

- Data are raw facts
- Information is the result of processing raw data to reveal meaning
- Information requires context to reveal meaning
- Raw data must be formatted for storage, processing, and presentation
- Data are the foundation of information, which is the bedrock of knowledge
- Data are building blocks of information
- Information is produced by processing data
- Accurate, relevant, timely information is the key to good decision making
- Good decision making is the key to organizational survival

1.2.4 Database

A database is defined as an organized collection of logically related (or interrelated) data. A database may be of any size and complexity. A database is organized in such a way that a computer program can quickly select desired pieces of data. A database consists of four elements – data, data relationships, data constraints (rules), and schema. In simple terms a database is a collection of interrelated data. Defining a database means specifying the data types, data structures and constraints (or conditions) of the data in the database.

A database is a collection of related information. Generally database describes the activities of one or more related organizations such as university, hospital, school, hostel, college, bank, research etc. Data are managed most efficiently when stored in a database. Database is a shared resource and it has integrated computer structure that stores a collection of data. A database is typically used to store the data. For example, a phone book is a database of names, addresses and phone numbers. For example, for the University related data means the collected or stored information such as Admissions, Departments, Students, Courses, Subjects, Hostels, Fee details, Faculty, Research, Students taking courses, Exams etc.

1.2.5 Data Dictionary

The descriptions of all objects that interact with the database are stored in the data dictionary. Data about data are called metadata. Metadata details are stored in data dictionary. Data dictionary is also known as data directory or system catalog or data repository or information repository. Data dictionary do not contain any data of the database. It is an effective tool for ensuring data consistency. Data dictionary is the key element of information resource management.

The information stored in the data dictionary can be directly accessed by database designers, users or DBAs when needed. Data dictionary stores the data that describes the database structure, constraints, applications, authorizations etc.

All relational DBMSs include a built in data dictionary that is frequently accessed and automatically updated by the RDBMS. This type of data dictionaries is called integrated data dictionaries. Third party data dictionaries used by DBAs are called standalone data dictionaries. Data dictionary stores all data details in the form of relational format. DBA can use the data dictionary to support data analysis and design. For query optimization DBMS accesses data dictionary.

Data dictionaries are divided into two types – active and passive. An active data dictionary is automatically updated by the DBMS whenever database access occurs so that data dictionary always contains up to date data. Whereas the passive data dictionary is not automatically updated, instead it is updated by running a batch process.

Data dictionary consists of the following items:

1. Description details of schemas of the database system
2. Descriptions of the database users, their responsibilities, and their access rights
3. Data usage standards
4. Application program descriptions
5. Database users details

6. A list of all files in the database.

7. The number of records in each file.

8. Names and data types of each field.

9. Name of the each relation.

10. Name of each field in the relation

11. Data type(integer, number, char, varcahar2, date, object etc) of each field in the relation

12. Length of each field

13. Detailed physical database design details such as data storage structures, data access paths, file sizes, record sizes, etc.

14. Default value of the field.

15. Whether the field is NULL or NOT NULL,

16. Constraints applicable to each field.

17. Data dictionary tells where a specific element is used, whom it is used etc

18. It stores details such as – relation creator, date of creation, number of columns of that relation, data access permissions of that relation, and other integrity constrains.

19. Indexes defined for each relation.

20. Relationships among all the data items.

21. Creator of the database, when the database is created, where the database is located,

1.2.6 Need of Database and DBMS

Database management systems (DBMS) are mainly used for effective and efficient management of large data. In order to survive in the competitive business environment effective and efficient information management is must for every organization. That is, database and database management systems (DBMSs) are inevitable for all organizations. Data sharing, easy data management, easy way of applying rules on data, data correctness, data consistency, are all advantages of database.

1.2.7 Definition of Database Management System (DBMS)

A database management system (DBMS) is a software system (set of programs) that is used to create and manage large databases efficiently and effectively. A DBMS provides a controlled and systematic method of creating, storing, updating (insertion, modification, deletion) and retrieving data in a database. A DBMS provides facilities such as data sharing, data controlling, data access, enforcing data integrity and security, managing concurrent data access, backup and recovery etc.

A DBMS is a collection of programs used to create, insert, modify, delete and query the data in the database. DBMS is general purpose software used to define, construct and update or manipulate data in the databases for different applications. Thus, a DBMS is a general purpose software package used for efficient and effective management of data in the computer. Structure of the data dictates the data model of the database.

A DBMS is a complex software system consisting of a number of software components. DBMSs ultimately stores data in the form of many many bits.

Database Management System (DBMS) is a software package to facilitate the creation and maintenance of a computerized database. DBMS is used to define, construct and manipulate data in the database. DBMS is a collection of programs that enables you to insert, modify, delete and extract information from a database. There are many different types of DBMSs, ranging from small database systems that run on personal computers to huge database systems that run on mainframes. The following are examples of database applications

1. Computerized library systems
2. Automated teller machines
3. Flight reservation systems
4. Railway reservation system
5. Computerized parts inventory systems
6. Accounting management

DBMS is the intermediary between the user and the database. DBMS enables data to be shared.

1.2.8 RDBMS

A DBMS that is based on relational data model is called relational database management system (RDBMS). RDBMS is a database management system based on relational data model defined by E.F.Codd. Data are stored in the form of rows and columns. A table is a collection of rows and columns. The relationships among tables are also stored in the form of the table.

1.2.9 Features of RDBMS – A typical RDBMS has the following features:

- Provides data to be stored in tables
- Persists data in the form of rows and columns (table)
- Provides primary key facility, to uniquely identify each row in the relation
- Creates indexes for quicker data retrieval
- Provides a virtual table creation in which sensitive data can be stored and simplified query can be applied.(views)
- Sharing a common column in two or more tables(primary key and foreign key)
- Provides multi user accessibility that can be controlled by individual users
- Provides a way to structure data as records, tables, or objects
- Accepts data input from operators and stores that data for later retrieval
- Provides query languages for searching, sorting, reporting, and other "decision support" activities that help users correlate and make sense of collected data
- Provides multiuser access to data, along with security features that prevent some users from viewing and/or changing certain types of information
- Provides data integrity features that prevent more than one user from accessing and changing the same information simultaneously
- Provides a data dictionary (metadata) that describes the structure of the database, related files, and record information

A database management system (DBMS) or relational database management system (RDBMS) is a software program that typically operates on a database server or mainframe system to manage structured data, accept queries from users, and respond to those queries. Both DBMSs and RDBMSs almost have many common features or characteristics.

1.2.10 Database System

DBMS software and the database put together are known as a database system. Database system is a collection of database, DBMS and Application Programs. That is, the DBMS software together with the data is called a database system. That is,

Database System = Database + DBMS + Database Application Programs

1.2.11 Database Application

A database application is an application program or a set of related programs that is used by database users to perform a sequence of database operations such as create, insert, modify, delete and query etc. Databases are developed for management of data operations of Banks, Universities, Railways, Airlines, Libraries etc.

1.2.12 Data Sharing

Data sharing is a primary feature of a database management system (DBMS).

Main advantage of data sharing is the ability to share the same data resource with multiple applications or users. It implies that the data are stored in one or more servers in the network and that there is some software locking mechanism that prevents the same set of data from being changed by two people at the same time.

Sharing database with other users on a network is easy - just place the folder containing the database file onto a networked drive. Anyone who has access to the drive will be able to retrieve both the text information as well as the diagrams, images. You can set password and user access privileges to the database through your network security administration.

1.2.13 Database Security

To protect the database we must apply various security measures at several levels such as operating system level, physical level, database system level, network etc.

Database maintenance is under the control of the DBA. The DBA has the ultimate responsibility for the data management in the database. DBA has to choose the best file structures and access methods to get optimal performance of the system by eliminating or resolving the conflicting requirements of various users and applications. DBA is responsible for implementing measures for ensuring the security, integrity, and recovery of the database.

1.2.14 Database Integrity

Data integrity means that the data contained in the database is both accurate and consistent. Another integrity check of the database is to ensure that if there is a reference to certain object, that object must exist.

SQL DDL includes commands for specifying data integrity constraints on the data in the database. An integrity constraint is a condition specified on the database scheme for restricting the data to be stored in the relations.

Data integrity refers to correctness of data stored in the database. Data values stored in the database must be correct before and after the modification of database.

Data values in the database must satisfy certain conditions. By using DBMS it is very easy to enforce data integrity constraints on the data stored in the database.

The DBA is responsible for implementing procedures for ensuring the security, integrity and recovery of the database.

Database integrity involves the correctness of data stored in the database. Data correctness (database integrity) has to be preserved in the presence of concurrent database operations, errors in the users operations and application programs, and failures in hardware and software.

1.3 Types of Database Users

1.3.1 Database Designers

Responsible for designing the database, identifying the data to be stored in the database and for choosing appropriate structure to represent and store the data. It is the responsibility of database designers to communicate with all prospective of the database users in order to understand their requirements so that they can create a design that meets user requirements.

1.3.2 Database Administrators (DBAs)

The DBA is a person or a group of persons who is responsible for the management of the database. The DBA is responsible for authorizing access to the database by grant and revoke permissions to the users, for coordinating and monitoring its use, managing backups and repairing damage due to hardware and/or software failures and for acquiring hardware and software resources as needed. In case of small organization the role of DBA is performed by a single person and in case of large organizations there is a group of DBAs who share responsibilities. That is DBAs are responsible for managing the database system, authorizing access, revoking access coordinating and monitoring users, acquiring resources when required.

1.3.3 Application Programmers

Application Programmers are responsible for writing application programs that use data stored in the database. These programs could be written in General Purpose Programming languages such as Visual Basic, Forms Developer, C, FORTRAN, COBOL etc. to manipulate the data stored in the database. These application programs operate on the data stored in the database to perform various operations such as retaining information, creating new information, deleting or changing existing information in the database.

1.3.4 End Users

The persons that use the database for querying, updating (insert, update, and delete), and generating reports, etc. End Users are the people who interact with the database through database applications or utilities. The various categories of end users are given below:

- Casual End Users – These Users occasionally access the database but may need different information each time. They use sophisticated Database Query Language to specify their requests. For example: High level or middle level Managers who access the data weekly or biweekly. Casual end users also known as occasional users

- Native End Users – These users frequently query and update the database using standard types of Queries. The operations that can be performed by this class of users are very limited and affect precise portion of the database.

    For example: Reservation clerks for airlines/hotels check availability for given request and make reservations. Also, persons using Automated Teller Machines (ATM's) fall under this category as he has access to limited portion of the database.

- Standalone end Users/On-line End Users – Those end users who interact with the database directly via on-line terminal or indirectly through menu or graphics based Interfaces.

    For example: User of a text package, library management software that store variety of library data such as issue and return of books for fine purposes.

- Parametric (or naive) end users: They use pre-programmed transactions to interact continuously with the database. For example, bank tellers or reservation clerks.

- Sophisticated end users: Use full DBMS capabilities for implementing complex applications.

1.3.5 System Analysts

Design and implement transactions for users. Design and implement the DBMS software package itself.

1.36 Tool developers

Design and implement tools that facilitate the use of the DBMS software. Tools include design tools, performance tools, special interfaces, etc.

1.37 Operators and maintenance personnel

Work on running and maintaining the hardware and software environment for the database system.

1.4 Evolution of Database Management Systems (DBMSs)

In 1960s Database management systems were first introduced during 1960s. File processing systems were so popular.

1970s Hierarchical and network database management systems were developed. Hierarchical and network database management systems were considered as first generation DBMS.

Problems with hierarchical and network DBMs are

- Very limited data independence
- Very difficult to access data
- Data were isolated

1980s A relational data model was developed. Relational data model is a second generation DBMS.

- All data are represented in the form of tables.
- Very easy to access data.
- Very easy to represent relationships among data items.
- Well suited for clients/servers computing, parallel processing, and graphical interfaces.

1990s third generation object oriented DBMS were developed. Data warehousing and Internet application were introduced.

2000 and after 2000

Object relational, web based models, data warehousing, multidimensional data models and other advanced data models were developed. These models are:

- Easy to manage complex data types such as multidimensional data.
- Increases usage of internet applications.
- Distributed database systems were developed.

16

- Content addressable storage becomes more popular. It searches data rather than memory location.
- Intelligent systems were developed using artificial intelligence
- Data mining techniques were introduced
- Pervasive devices were introduced.
- Increased usage of web services.

1.5 Disadvantages or Problems With Conventional File Oriented (Processing) Systems

The conventional file processing system suffers from the following shortcomings (disadvantages or pitfalls).

1.5.1 Data redundancy or data duplication

Data redundancy means same information is duplicated in several files. This makes data redundancy. That is, same data values are stored in many locations or places in the secondary memory such as hard disk, magnetic tape, etc. It is called data duplication or data redundancy or repetition of data. It causes data maintenance (insert, modify, and delete) problems or anomalies. Lot of redundancy is there in conventional file processing systems.

COBOL, third generation high level computer programming language is an excellent example for file processing system for business applications. COBOL was mainly used for business applications. Abbreviation of COBOL is common business oriented language. COBOL uses files for data management. Data management means applying data manipulation operations on data such as inserting, updating, and deleting.

1.5.2 Data Inconsistency

Data inconsistency means different copies of the same data are not matching. That means different versions of same basic data are existing. This occurs as the result of update operations that are not updating the same data stored at different places or locations of the secondary memory.

Example: Address information of a customer is recorded differently in different files.

1.5.3 Difficulty in Accessing Data

It is not easy to retrieve information using a conventional file processing system. Convenient and efficient information retrieval is almost impossible using conventional file processing system.

1.5.4 Data Isolation

Data are scattered in various files, and the files may be in different formats, writing new application programs to retrieve data is very difficult.

1.5.5 Integrity Problems

The data values may need to satisfy some integrity constraints. For example the balance field value in the customer account details must be greater than Rs 2600. We have to handle this through program code in file processing systems. But in database systems we can declare the integrity constraints along with definition itself.

1.5.6 Atomicity Problem

It is difficult to ensure atomicity property in file processing system. For example, transferring an amount of $123 from an account A to account B, if a failure occurs during execution there could be situation like $123 is deducted from Account A and not credited in Account B.

1.5.7 Concurrent Access anomalies

If multiple users are updating the same data stored in the database simultaneously it will result in inconsistent data state. In file processing system it is very difficult to handle this using program code. This results in concurrent access anomalies. There are many advantages of concurrent data processing. Some of the advantages are given below:

1. Resource sharing (CPU, memory, hard disk, etc)
2. Increased throughput
3. Data sharing

1.5.8 Security Problems

Enforcing security constraints in file processing system is very difficult as the application programs are added to the system in an ad-hoc manner.

1.5.9 Program data dependence

File descriptions such as file type, field names, field types, field lengths are stored in the application program that accesses a specified file. If file details are changed then program must be modified and vice versa.

1.5.10 Limited data sharing

Every application program has its own private files and it is not possible to share the outside files.

1.5.11 Lengthy program development times

In traditional file processing system all application programs are developed independently every time from scratch file formats, file descriptions and file access logic are designed separately from scratch every time.

1.5.12 Very high program maintenance

More than 80% program maintenance is more than 80% of the total information systems development budget.

In simple terms advantages and disadvantages of file processing and database approach are given below:

Disadvantages of file Processing System (FPS)	Advantages of Database Approach (DBMS)
1. Program-data dependence	1. Program-data independence
2. Duplication of data	2. Planned data redundancy
3. Limited data sharing	3. Improved data sharing
4. Lengthy development times	4. Increased productivity of application development
5. Excessive program maintenance	5. Reduced program maintenance
6. Limited data consistency	6. Improved data consistency
7. Difficult to enforce standards	7. Enforcement of standards
8. Limited data quality	8. Improved data quality
9. Limited data accessibility and responsiveness	9. Improved data accessibility and responsiveness
10. Limited decision support	10. Improved decision support
11. Limited backup and recovery	11. Many backup and recovery tasks are automated

1.6 Advantages of Database Management Systems (DBMS)

1.6.1 Program-Data Independence

Separately storing and managing of data descriptions from the application programs that use the data is called data-independence. Changes in application programs do not affect changes in data and vice versa. The data is held in such a way that changes to the structure of the database do not affect any of the programs used to access the data.

1.6.2 Controlled data redundancy

Storing of same data in many locations in the database is called data redundancy. Best method is to store one fact (one value) in one place in the database. It may not be possible to eliminate hundred percent data redundancies. Existing data redundancies must be controlled in a systematic way.

1.6.3 Improved data consistency

Data consistency means, data must always be correct in the database before and after modification of data in the database.

1.6.4 Improved data sharing

Many database users are allowed to share the data stored in the database. A database is designed as a shared corporate resource.

1.6.5 Increased productivity of application development

Database approach greatly reduces the cost and time for developing new business applications. That is, development of application software is very fast and cheap.

1.6.6 Reduced program maintenance

Change in data formats and access methods, adding new data item types, adding primary key foreign key and unique key are very easy in database approach. Many tasks are performed automatically.

1.6.7 Enforcement of standards

Establishing and enforcing data standards is very easy. Standards such as data quality standards, naming conventions, uniform procedures for accessing, inserting, modifying, deleting, querying and protecting data can be applied very easily with database approach. Also many software tools are available for implementing various standards on the data stored in the database.

1.6.8 Improved data quality

Best tools, good procedures, processes and rules are available in database approach to improve the data quality.

1.6.9 Improved data accessibility and responsiveness

It is very easy to access data in the database by using high level fourth generation languages such as structured query language (SQL), Datalog, Quel etc.

1.6.10 Improved decisions support

Very easy to develop decision support applications for accurate decision making.

1.7 DBMS Additional Advantages

1. Greater flexibility
2. Good for larger databases
3. Greater processing power
4. Fits the needs of many medium to large-sized organizations
5. Storage for all relevant data
6. Provides user views relevant to tasks performed
7. Provides backup and recovery controls
8. Advanced security and integrity
9. The data can be shared.
10. Redundancy can be reduced or controlled the redundancy means storing the same data in the database multiple times and it leads to several problems
11. Inconsistency can be avoided
12. Transaction support can be provided
13. Integrity can be maintained

Most database applications have certain integrity constraints that must hold for the data. A DBMS should provide capabilities for defining and enforcing these constraints.

14. Security can be enforced
15. Conflicting requirements can be balanced. Standards can be enforced
16. Representing complex relationships among data A database may include numerous varieties of data that are interrelated in many ways.
17. Providing database backup and recovery a DBMS must provide facilities for recovering from hardware or software failures.

1.8 DBMS Disadvantages

1. Difficult to learn
2. High cost of DBMS

A complete database management system is very large and sophisticated software. It is expensive to purchase database management software

3. Requires skilled administrators
4. Slower processing speeds
5. Higher Hardware Cost

Database management systems (DBMSs) are very complicated and very large software systems. Additional memory and processing power may be required to run the database management systems (DBMS). It may require more powerful hardware and operating systems and many other software tools.

6. Higher Programming

DBMS is complex software with many features. The programmers need a thorough knowledge of database management system (DBMS) to use it to best advantage. If the organization hires experienced database programmers, it has to pay extra cost for their expertise.

7. Higher Conversion Cost

If an organization converts its records to database management system, data has to be converted from files to the database system. Because of the different formats used by different systems, this may be a difficult and time-consuming process. Moreover, the structure and data may also have to be modified according to the requirements of the database management system.

8. More Chance of Failure

In database management system (DBMS), all resources and components are centralized. If any of these components fails, the whole database management system (DBMS) stops.

9. Complexity and Performance

Database management system is general-purpose software. A complete DBMS has to perform many tasks that make it complex and complicated software. In some applications, DBMS may run less efficiently as compared to file processing system.

1.9 Major Components in a Database System Environment

1.9.1 DBMS

A DBMS is a complex software system consisting of a number of components. It is software system that is used to create, insert, modify, delete and query the data in the database. DBMS provides controlled access to user databases.

1.9.2 Database

A database is an organized collection of logically related (or interrelated) data, usually designed to meet the information needs of multiple users in an organization.

Collection of facts are stored in the database. Database may contain either data or information or both.

1.9.3 Data Repository or Data Dictionary (DD)

It contains meta data. Data about data is called Meta data. It is also called data dictionary (DD) or data directory or data catalog. It contains details such as data item names, relationships, primary keys, foreign keys etc.

1.9.4 Database Application Programs

Computer programs that are used to create and maintain data in the databases and provide information to users.

1.9.5 Computer-aided software engineering(CASE)tools

CASE tools are automated tools used to design databases and application programs.

1.9.6 User Interface

Users will use menus, icons, language and other facilities to interact with database system components such as DBMS, repository, CASE tools, application programs, end users etc.

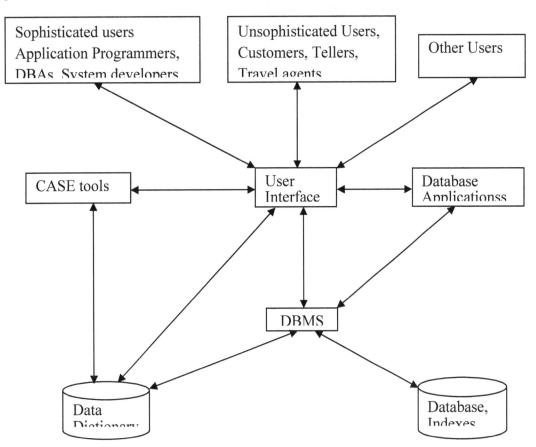

Figure1.1   Major Components in a database system environment

Important components of a database system environment are shown in the Figure1.1

1.9.7 Data and Database Administrators

Data administrator is responsible for management of data resources in the entire organization. Database administrators (DBAs) are responsible for database design, security, integrity, controlling data access etc.

1.9.8 System Developers

Programmers, system analysts, module leaders, project leaders who are responsible for design and develop new application software.

1.9.9 End Users

Persons who add, modify, delete and query the data in the database.

1.9.10 Hardware

  i. Computers,

  ii. Peripherals and

  iii. Networked devices.

1.9.11 Software

- Operating systems software, DBMS software

- Applications programs and utilities software

1.9.12 People

- Systems administrators,

- Database administrators (DBAs)

- Database designers, systems analysts and programmers, End users

1.9.13 Procedures

Instructions and rules that govern the design and use of the database system.

1.9.14 Database and Indexes

Database is a collection of interrelated information of a specific organization. Indexes are used to speed up the data retrieval process. There exist different types of indexes such as primary index, clustered index, un-clustered index, B+ tree index, secondary indexes, and hash indexes used for different data access operations of the data stored in the database

1.10 Architecture or Structure of DBMS or Major components of DBMS

Functional components of a DBMS are divided into:

1. Query processor components (or Query management)

- DDL compiler
- DML compiler
- Query evaluation engine
2. Storage manager components
   - Data security and integrity manager
   - Files and data access manager
   - Transaction manager
   - Database recovery manager
   - Buffer manager
   - Disk space manager
3. Data structures for physical DBMS implementation
   - Database files
   - System catalog or Data dictionary
   - Indexes
   - Statistical data

DDL compiler

DDL compiler interprets DDL statements and then stores them in data dictionary for future management.

DML compiler

DML compiler compiles and executes all data manipulation statements such as insert, update, delete, and query statements. It also finds best strategy for query execution.

Query evaluation engine

Query evaluation engine acts as an interface between DML compiler and lower level storage manager component.

Data security and integrity manager

Data security and integrity manager controls database access permissions of users and checks integrity details of various values in the database system.

Files and data access manager

Responsible for files creation, modification, and deletion. It also manages various file access methods.

Transaction manager

It is responsible for executing all transactions including serial and concurrent transactions. Also responsible for ensuring consistency of data in the database against all system failures.

Disk space manager

It manages space on disk. It supports the concept of page as a unit of data on the disk for reading and writing. It manages data as a collection of pages.

Buffer manager

It is responsible for fetching data from disk to main memory (RAM). Also responsible for maintaining the desired data in the cache memory.

Database recovery manager

Responsible for maintaining database logs and restoring the database system to a consistent state after crashes.

Data dictionary

Data dictionary is also known as data directory or system catalog. It stores metadata. Data about data is called metadata. It stores all relations names, attribute names, data types of each attribute, lengths of fields, primary key, foreign key, unique etc.

Indexes

Indexes are useful for speeding up data searching capabilities in database. Different types of indexing techniques are available in DBMS. Some indexing techniques are – Primary index, secondary index, clustering index, Bitmap indexes, B+ tree indexes, Hash indexes etc.

Statistical data

Statistical information details of data in the database are stored in statistical data structures. It is useful for finding best or efficient query execution strategy

Database

Full data details of a particular organization or organizations are stored in the database.

1.11 Database development using Three Schema Architecture or Data abstraction levels in a DBMS

The three schemas architecture is used to describe the structure of the database. The three schemas are only descriptions of data but actual data exists only at physical schema or physical level. Three schemas of the database are given below:

1. External Schema or external view or external level or user view
2. Conceptual Schema or conceptual view or conceptual level
3. Internal Schema or internal view or internal level

External Schemas

A database may have many external schemas. Each external schema is a collection of one or more relations and zero or more views. A view is similar to a relation but the records of the view are not stored in the database. A view is a stored query. For different individual users or groups of users data access permissions on parts of a database are given. External schemas are custom designed schemas based on the requirements of the end users of the database system.

There exist many external schemas for a single database. External schemas are also known as user views. Each external schema describes the part of the database belonging to a particular user or users group. It is at highest level of database abstraction. For a given conceptual view there may exists many user views. It helps to ensure database security. It makes database application development easier.

Conceptual Schema

A high level data model is used for describing the conceptual schema. It hides physical storage details of the database. It represents database entities and the relationships among them. The most widely used conceptual model is the entity relationship (ER) model. External views are integrated into a single conceptual view. It is independent of both hardware and software.

Internal Schema

Internal schema consists of two separate schemas :

1. Logical schema and
2. Physical schema.

The logical schema is represented in the selected database model of the DBMS. Relational data model (RDM) is the standard, popular, famous, convenient, useful, and default logical data model. In RDBMS the logical schema describes all relations stored in the database.

The physical schema of the database describes how data are actually stored in secondary memory using a particular DBMS such as Oracle or DB2 or Ms SQL Server, Sybase, MYSQL, TeraData, Ingress, Informix, MS Access, etc. The physical schema describes file organizations, record formats, types of indexes, etc. There is one physical schema for each logical schema. Physical schema describes the physical storage structure of the database. It operates at the lowest level of database abstraction. It is dependent on the selected DBMS.

Physical schema describes or specifies how data is actually stored on the secondary storage devices such as disks and magnetic tapes. Designing file organizations to store relations, creating indexes to speed up data retrieval or query operations.

1.12 Data Independence

Data Independence

Data independence is defined as the ability or capability to modify the database schema details at a particular level without affecting or creating any problems in the database schema details of the higher levels. Data independence is a powerful feature of a database system.

There are two types of data independencies:

1. Physical data independence and
2. logical data independence

Physical Data Independence

Physical data independence allows changes in the physical storage devices or changes in the organization of the files or indexes creation or deletion or modification and record modification without requiring any changes in the conceptual and external higher levels. The files may migrate from one type of physical media to another physical media or the file structure may change without any need for changes in the application programs.

Logical Data Independence

Logical data independence is the ability to modify the conceptual schema without creating any problem in external levels or external views. That is, if some fields or added in conceptual level there will not be any problem in external levels. Also it is possible to delete or modify fields at conceptual level when the fields are not used in external levels.

1.13 Self Assessment Questions

1.13.1 Short Answer Questions:

1. What is data?
2. What is information?
3. Differentiate between data and information?
4. What is database?
5. What are the advantages of data sharing?
6. What is database application?
7. List different users of database.
8. Define DBMS
9. What are the features of RDBMS?
10. What is data dictionary?
11. What is data independence?

1.13.2 Essay Type Questions

1. Differentiate file processing approach and database approach
2. What are the advantages of database management systems (DBMS)?
3. Explain the evolution of database management systems (DBMSs)
4. Explain components of a database system environment.
5. Explain major components of DBMS.
6. Explain three schema architecture of a database system.
7. Explain different data independences.

CHAPTER 2
DATABASE MODELS

Objectives

- ✓ To know about database models
- ✓ To study database models
- ✓ To understand classification or categorization of database models
- ✓ To study database modeling
- ✓ To learn about conceptual, logical, and physical database models

Chapter Structure

2.1   Introduction

2.2   Definition of Data Model

2.3   Database Models

2.4   Types or Categories of Database Models

2.5   Data Modeling

2.6   Self Assessment Questions

2.1 Introduction

A database model fundamentally determines in which manner data can be stored, organized, and manipulated in a database system. The purpose of a database model is to represent data in the database and to make the data understandable. A database model describes how a database is structured and used. A database model is a collection of concepts for describing data. It is a way of storing and retrieving data in the database. A database model is a theory or specification describing how a database is structured and used. Several such models have been suggested. The most popular example of a database model is the relational model.

Database modeling is used for representing entities of interest and their relationships in the database. Most data representation models provide mechanisms to structure data for the entities being modeled and allow a set of operations to be defined on them. The models can also enforce a set of constraints to maintain data integrity.

A data model is not just a way of structuring data: it also defines a set of operations that can be performed on the data. The relational data model, for example, defines operations such as select, project and join. Although these operations may not be explicit in a particular query language, they provide the foundation on which a query language is built.

Various techniques are used to model data structure. Most database systems are built around one particular data model, although it is possible for products to offer support for more than one model. For any logical model various physical implementations may be possible, and most products will offer the user some level of control in tuning the physical implementation, since the choices that are made have a significant effect on performance.

2.2 Definition of Data Model

Data Model can be defined as an integrated collection of concepts for describing and manipulating data, relationships between data, and constraints on the data in an organization. That is, a database model is defined as collection of concepts, ideas, plans to define data types, to create relationships, and to specify constraints on the data in the database. Database model describes and explains how data is structured in the database. Database models also specify basic operations such as insert, modify, delete and retrieval of data in the database.

2.3 Database Models

Database systems can be based on different data models or database models respectively. A data model is a collection of concepts and rules for the description of the structure of the database. Structure of the database means the data types, the constraints and the relationships for the description or storage of data respectively.

A model is a representation of reality, 'real world' objects and events, and their associations. It is an abstraction that concentrates on the essential, inherent aspects of an organization and ignores the other properties. A data model represents the organization itself. Data model provides the basic concepts and notations that will allow database designers and end users unambiguously and accurately to communicate their understanding of the organizational data.

A data model comprises of three components:

1. A structural part, consisting of a set of rules according to which databases can be constructed.

2. A manipulative part. Defining the types of operation that are allowed on the data (this includes the operations that are used or updating or retrieving data from the database and for changing the structure of the database).

3. Possibly a set of integrity rules, which ensures that the data is accurate.

2.4 Types or Categories of Database Models

Database models are classified into three categories:-

1. High-level (or Conceptual) Database Models.
2. Representational (or Implementation) Database Models.
3. Low-Level (or Physical) Database Models.

2.4.1 High-level (or Conceptual) Data Models

Conceptual data models use concepts such as entities, attributes, and relationships, specialization, generalization etc. between (or among) entities. Entity relationship(ER) data model is a very high level conceptual data model. Other conceptual database models are – enhanced entity relationship (EER) database model, and unified markup language (UML) database model.

2.4.2 Representational (or Implementation) Data Models.

Relational, hierarchical, network data models are example for implementation data models. These data models are also called record based data model because data are represented by using records (or rows)

Object data models and object relational-data models are latest implementation data models. Object-relational data models are also known as extended-relational data models. Object data model defines a database in terms of objects, their properties and their operations.

2.4.3 Low-Level (or Physical) Data Models

Physical data models describe how data are actually stored in the computers storage devices such as magnetic disk, magnetic tape etc. Physical data model describes details such as record formats, record types, index details, type of index, file types, file formats, and pages etc.

A data model of the DBMS hides many complex details, such a data model is a collection of high level data description constructs. A database model is used to define the structure of a database. A data model is defined as collection of conceptual tools that are used to describe data to explain relationships among data and consistency constraints on data.

2.4.4 Common database models or record based or representational database models include:

1. Hierarchical Data Model
2. Network Data Model
3. Relational Data Model
4. Object Data Model
5. Object-Relational Data Model
6. Hybrid Database Model
7. Multidimensional Data Model (MDDB)

1. Hierarchical Data Model

It represents parent child relationships from parent entity set to child entity sets. Hierarchical database schema defines a tree data structure. That is, the hierarchical data model organizes data in a tree structure. A parent child relationship is one-to-many(1: N) from parent to child records. Main data structuring concepts used in hierarchical data modeling are records and parent child relationship. Each occurrence or instance consists of one parent record and zero or more child records. There is a hierarchy of parent and child records. The employee and children data forms a hierarchy, where the employee data represents the parent record and the children data represents the child records. If an employee has three children, then there would be three child records associated with one employee record.

A hierarchical database schema consists of a number of hierarchical schemas. Each hierarchical schema or hierarchy consists of a number of record types and parent child relationships. A hierarchical schema is displayed as a hierarchical diagram, in which record set names are displayed in rectangular boxes and parent child relationships are displayed as lines connecting the parent's record set to the child record set. A record is a collection of fields or data items. Similar records are grouped into record types or record sets. To create links between records, the hierarchical model uses Parent Child Relationships. These are a 1: N (one-to-many) mapping between records. This restricts a child record to have only one parent record.

2. Network Data Model

The network model permits modeling of many-to-many, one-to-many, and one-to-one relationships in data. Concepts used in network data model are two data structures – records and sets. A many-to-many relationship (M;N) exists between two entity sets or entity types STUDENTS and EXAMS. A network database is a collection of set occurrences or set instances corresponding to a set type. Each set instance relates one record from the owner record type to many records of member record type. Set instance maintains a 1:N relationship from owner to member. Network model organizes data using two fundamental constructs, called records and sets. Records contain fields, and sets define one-to-many relationships between records: one owner, many members.

A field is the basic unit of information. A record is a collection of fields. Collection of similar records is called entity type. A network database is a collection of entity types. A set type is a description of a 1:N relationship between two record types. Definition of each set type has three basic elements:

1. A name for the set type
2. An owner record type
3. A member record type

Some data were more naturally modeled with more than one parent per child. The basic data modeling construct in the network model is the set construct. A set consists of an owner record type, a set name, and a member record type. A member record type can have that role in more than one set, hence the multi-parent concept is supported. An owner record type can also be a member or owner in another set. The data model is a simple network, and link and intersection record types may exist, as well as sets between them. Thus, the complete network of relationships is represented by several pair wise sets; in each set some (one) record type is owner (at the tail of the network arrow) and one or more record types are members (at the head of the relationship arrow). Usually, a set defines a 1:M relationship, although 1:1 is permitted.

3. Relational Data Model (RDM)

One of the reasons behind the success of relational model is its simplicity.

The first of three main database architectures is the relational database. The vast majority of databases are of this sort. Relational databases store data in a row and column model, much like a spreadsheet. The individual columns are called fields, and the rows are called records. The entire collection of rows is usually referred to as a table. A new language, Structured Query Language (SQL) was created for working with this relational way of modeling data.

In relational data model, data and relationships between data are organized in tables. A table is a collection of records and each record in a table contains the same fields. RDBMS is a database management system based on the relational data model developed by E.F. Codd. An RDBMS allows the definition of data structures, storage and retrieval operations and integrity constraints.

Properties of Relational Tables

1. Values Are Atomic
2. Each Row is Unique
3. Column Values Are of the Same Kind
4. The Sequence of Columns is Insignificant
5. The Sequence of Rows is Insignificant
6. Each Column Has a Unique Name

Certain fields may be designated as keys, which mean that searches for specific values of that field will use indexing to speed them up. Where fields in two different tables take values from the same set, a join operation can be performed to select related records in the two tables by matching values in those fields. Often, but not always, the fields will have the same name in both tables.

The relational data model was introduced as a way to make DBMSs more independent of any particular application. It is a mathematical model defined in terms of predicate logic and set theory. Three key terms are used extensively in relational database models: relations, attributes, and domains. A relation is a table with columns and rows. The named columns of the relation are called attributes, and the domain is the set of values in which the attributes are allowed to take.

The basic data structure of the relational model is the table, where information about a particular entity (say, student) is represented in rows (also called tuples or records) and columns. A relation is a set of tuples. All relations in a relational database have to satisfy some basic rules to qualify as relations. First, the ordering of columns is immaterial in a table. Second, there can't be identical tuples or rows in a table. And third, each tuple will contain a single value for each of its attributes.

A relational database contains multiple tables. A key that can be used to uniquely identify a row in a table is called a primary key. Keys are commonly used to join or combine data from two or more tables. Keys are also critical in the creation of indexes, which facilitate fast retrieval of data from large relations. Any column can be a key, or multiple columns can be grouped together into a compound key. It is not necessary to define all the keys in advance; a column can be used as a key even if it was not originally intended to be one.

A key that has an external, real-world meaning (such as a book's ISBN, or a car's serial number) is sometimes called a "natural" key. If no natural key is suitable (think of the many people named "RAMA"), an arbitrary or surrogate key can be assigned (such as by giving employees ID numbers).

Relational data model is the best known and in today's DBMS most often implemented database model. It defines a database as a collection of tables (relations) which contain all data.

4. Object-Oriented Data Model (OODM)

Object-oriented models define a database as a collection of objects with features and methods. It contains collection of objects. Many objects can be created from the same class. An object contains data and methods to operate on the data. The relational data model and ER models are not sufficient to model the data requirements of some new database applications. Data types available in relational data model are not sufficient for many modern database applications such as CAD, CAM, etc. object data model and object query languages are also available. Database systems developed based on object oriented-data model are called object oriented database management systems (OODBMS). The rich data types in OODBMS offer a database designer many opportunities for a more natural or more efficient design.

Object oriented database management systems (OODBMS) are developed based on the object oriented data model. OODBMS have the capability of representing complex objects and the operations on those objects. Usage of object-oriented programming languages increasing fastly. Many commercial object oriented DBMSs are currently available. Many object oriented DBMSs use object oriented features such as polymorphism, encapsulation, inheritance, operator overloading, dynamic binding etc.

Every object has two components – value and operation OODBMSs model real–world objects more closely. An object can have a complex data structure. In object oriented programming languages an object exists only during program execution that is why they are called transient objects. In OODBMS objects are stored permanently in secondary storage and these objects are sharable among multiple programs and applications. An object may have an object structure of arbitrary complexity in order to represent all of the necessary information for object description.

In OODBMS for each object a unique identity called object identifier (OID) is generated and assigned by the system. The OID value should not change for a particular object, this is called immutable. An object definition language (ODL) is used to define object.

The second major type of DBMS is object-oriented. This type stores objects rather than records. The objects it stores are like Java classes--a combination of both data and methods for manipulating that data. This is very different than the relational approach, where you only store the data, and the manipulation of that data is left to a procedural process. The object-oriented type of DBMS is typically not supported by JDBC.

Object DBMSs add database functionality to object programming languages. They bring much more than persistent storage of programming language objects. Object DBMSs extend the semantics of the C++, Smalltalk and Java object programming languages to provide full-featured database programming capability, while retaining native language compatibility. A major benefit of this approach is the unification of the application and database development into a seamless data model and language environment. As a result, applications require less code, use more natural data modeling, and code bases are easier to maintain. Object developers can write complete database applications with a modest amount of additional effort.

"The object-oriented database (OODB) paradigm is the combination of object-oriented programming language (OOPL) systems and persistent systems. The power of the OODB comes from the seamless treatment of both persistent data, as found in databases, and transient data, as found in executing programs."

In contrast to a relational DBMS where a complex data structure must be flattened out to fit into tables or joined together from those tables to form the in-memory structure, object DBMSs have no performance overhead to store or retrieve a web or hierarchy of interrelated objects.

This one-to-one mapping of object programming language objects to database objects has two benefits over other storage approaches: it provides higher performance management of objects, and it enables better management of the complex interrelationships between objects. This makes object DBMSs better suited to support applications such as financial portfolio risk analysis systems, telecommunications service applications, world wide web document structures, design and manufacturing systems, and hospital patient record systems, which have complex relationships between data.

5. Object-Relational Data Model (ORDBMS)

Database systems developed based on object-relational data model are called object relational database management systems (ORDBMS). Relational database management systems (RDBMSs) are extended by adding object features. In object database systems every object should have an object identifier (OID). Some main features of object relational database management systems (ORDBMS) are:

1. An ORDBMS allows us to design better databases.
2. OODBMS adds DBMS functionality to the already existing programming languages.
3. ORDBMS adds richer data types to RDBMS.

The third type of database is a hybrid of the previous two, called an object-relational database. It combines characteristics of both. Like relational systems, it might support the SQL language, and like object-oriented systems, it allows for the storage of objects. Often, relational database vendors will create extensions to their systems to support storing objects.

Object relational database management systems (ORDBMSs) add new object storage capabilities to the relational systems. These new facilities integrate management of complex objects such as time-series, geospatial data, and diverse binary media such as audio, video, images, and applets. By encapsulating methods with data structures, an ORDBMS server can execute complex analytical and data manipulation operations to search and transform multimedia and other complex objects.

As an evolutionary technology, the object relational approach has inherited the robust transaction- and performance-management features of its relational data model and the flexibility of its object-oriented features. Database designers can work with familiar tabular structures and data definition languages (DDLs) while assimilating new object-management possibilities.

Similar to a relational database model, but objects, classes and inheritance are directly supported in database schemas and in the query language.

Object-relational model and object-oriented models are very powerful but also quite complex. With the relatively new object-relational database model is the wide spread and simple relational database model extended by some basic object-oriented concepts. These allow us to work with the widely known relational database model but also have some advantages of the object-oriented model without its complexity.

6. Hybrid Database Model

A hybrid database is a combination of two or more database types and models. An emerging type of hybrid database is the hybrid XML/relational database, which is a type of database that can store and retrieve both XML and relational data. Both of the types of data can be accessed via queries and the databases can work together in a single database application.

7. Multidimensional Data Model (MDDB)

During the past decade, the multidimensional data model emerged for use when the objective is to analyze data rather than to perform online transactions. Multidimensional database technology is a key factor in the interactive analysis of large amounts of data for decision-making purposes. In contrast to previous technologies, these databases view data as multidimensional cubes that are particularly well suited for data analysis.

Multidimensional models categorize data either as facts with associated numerical measures or as textual dimensions that characterize the facts. In multidimensional data model normalization is not an important issue. Structuring is most important.

Multidimensional data models have three important application areas within data analysis. Data warehouses are large repositories that integrate data from several sources in an enterprise for analysis. Online analytical processing (OLAP) systems provide fast answers for queries that aggregate large amounts of detail data to find overall trends. Data mining applications seek to discover knowledge by searching semi automatically for previously unknown patterns and relationships in multidimensional databases.

Multidimensional databases are capable of storing, viewing and sorting the same data in different ways. It would seem feasible to use this method in a national sales environment where geographic regions, months, people and products vs. sales are tracked. Other databases may require the user to scroll through a long list or table, while MDDB's structured presentation enables all possible combinations of information to be viewed along one common dimensional position.

Star schema is the simplest style of data warehouse schema. The star schema consists of a few "fact tables" (possibly only one, justifying the name) referencing any number of "dimension tables". The star schema is considered an important special case of the snowflake schema.

2.5 Data Modeling

Data modeling is the process of defining real world phenomena or geographic features of interest in terms of their characteristics and their relationships with one another. It is concerned with different phases of work carried out to implement information organization and data structure.

- There are three steps in the data modeling process, resulting in a series of progressively formalized data models as the form of the database becomes more and more rigorously defined

  ❖ conceptual data modeling – defining in broad and generic terms the scope and requirements of a database.

  ❖ logical data modeling – specifying the user's view of the database with a clear definition of attributes and relationships.

  ❖ physical data modeling – specifying internal storage structure and file organization of the database.

- Data modeling is obviously closely related to the three levels of data abstraction in database design:

  ❖ conceptual data modeling ----> data model

  ❖ logical data modeling ---------> data structure

  ❖ physical data modeling -------> file structure

2.5.1 Conceptual Data Modeling

- entity-relationship (E-R) modeling is probably the most popular method of conceptual data modeling. Conceptual data modeling is sometimes referred to as a method of semantic data modeling because it used a human language-like vocabulary to describe information organization.

- Conceptual data modeling involves four aspects of work:

  ❖ Identifying entities-an entity is defined as a person, a place, an event, a thing, etc.

  ❖ Identifying attributes

  ❖ Determining relationships

  ❖ Drawing an entity-relationship diagram (E-R diagram)

2.5.2 Logical Data Modeling

- logical data modeling is a comprehensive process by which the conceptual data model is consolidated and refined

- The proposed database is reviewed in its entirety in order to identify potential problems such as

  ▪ irrelevant data that will not be used

  ▪ omitted or missing data

  ▪ inappropriate representation of entities

  ▪ lack of integration between various parts of the database

  ▪ unsupported applications

  ▪ potential additional cost to revise the database

  ▪ the end product of logical data modeling is a logical schema

  ▪ the logical schema is developed by mapping the conceptual data model (such as the E-R diagram) to a software-dependent design document

2.5.3 Physical Data Modeling

- physical data modeling is the database design process by which the actual tables that will be used to store the data are defined in terms of

  ○ data format --- the format of the data that is specific to a database management system (DBMS)

  ○ storage requirements --- the volume of the database

- physical location of data --- optimizing system performance by minimizing the need to transmit data between different storage devices or data servers
- the end product of physical data modeling is a physical schema
  - a physical schema is also variably known as data dictionary, item definition table, data specific table or physical database definition
  - it is both software- and hardware specific
  - this means the physical schemas for different systems look different from one another

2.6 Self Assessment Questions

2.6.1 Short Answer Questions

1. Define database model
2. What are the components of a database model?
3. What are the advantages of database models?
4. What are three steps in the data modeling process?
5. What is relational data model? Explain.
6. What are conceptual database models?
7. What are logical database models?
8. What is physical database modeling?

2.6.2 Essay Questions

1. Explain in detail different categories of database models

CHAPTER 3
DATABASE ENVIRONMENT

Objectives

- ✓ To understand the need of DBMSs in the organizations
- ✓ To know about strategic database planning
- ✓ To understand database management control
- ✓ To study the information domain of an organization
- ✓ To assess risks and costs of DBMSs

Chapter Structure

3.1   Database Systems in the Organization

3.2   Strategic Database Planning

3.3   Database and Management Control

3.4   The Information Domain

3.5   Risks and Costs of Database Management Systems (DBMSs)

3.6   Self Assessment Questions

3.1 Database Systems in The Organization

A database management system (DBMS) is computer software designed for the purpose of managing large databases in the organizations. Relational database management systems (RDBMSs) are the most popularly used database management systems in many organizations. Typical examples of RDBMSs include Oracle, Sybase, Informix, Ingress, DB2, Microsoft SQL Server, MySQL, Teradata, FileMaker and MS Access. RDBMSs are typically used by database administrators (DBAs) in the creation of database systems.

A DBMS is a complex set of software programs that controls the organization, storage and retrieval of data in a database. A DBMS includes: A modeling language to define the schema of each database hosted in the DBMS, according to the DBMS data model. The three most common data organizations are the hierarchical, network and relational data models. The most suitable structure depends on the application and on the transaction rate and the number of inquiries that will be made. The dominant model in use today is the relational data model (RDM).

Many DBMSs also support the Open Database Connectivity API that supports a standard way for programmers to access the DBMS. Data structures (fields, records and

43

files) optimized to deal with very large amounts of data stored on a permanent data storage device. A database query language and report writer to allow users to interactively interrogate the database, analyze its data and update it according to the users privileges on data.

DBMS also controls the security of the database. Data security prevents unauthorized users from viewing or updating the database. Using passwords, users are allowed access to the entire database or subsets of it called subschema. For example, an employee database can contain all the data about an individual employee, but one group of users may be authorized to view only payroll data, while others are allowed access to only work history and medical data.

If the DBMS provides a way to interactively enter and update the database, as well as querying the database, this capability allows for managing personal databases. However, it may not leave an audit trail of actions or provide the kinds of controls necessary in a multi-user organization. These controls are only available when a set of application programs are customized for each data entry and updating function.

A transaction mechanism, that ideally would guarantee the ACID properties, in order to ensure data integrity, despite concurrent user accesses (concurrency control), and faults (fault tolerance). DBMS also maintains the integrity of the data in the database. The DBMS can maintain the integrity of the database by not allowing more than one user to update the same record at the same time. The DBMS can help prevent duplicate records via unique index constraints; for example, no two customers with the same customer numbers (key fields) can be entered into the database. The DBMS accepts requests for data from the application program and instructs the operating system to transfer the appropriate data.

Organizations may use one kind of DBMS for daily transaction processing and then move the detail onto another computer that uses another DBMS better suited for random inquiries and analysis. Overall systems design decisions are performed by data administrators and systems analysts. Detailed database design is performed by database administrators. When a DBMS is used, information systems can be changed much more easily as the organization's information requirements change. New categories of data can be added to the database without disruption to the existing system.

Data is an important asset for any organization. Data are used by different people in different departments for different reasons in different organizations. Information is the backbone of any organization. Information is critical factor that enables managers and organizations to gain a competitive advantage. It is the indispensable link that ties together all the components of an organization for better operation, coordination and survival in the competitive environment.

In any organization future management is most important. Managing the future means managing the information. Hence getting the right information, in the right time in the right way is not an easy task. So, organizations will survive for a long term only when information is managed properly and correctly. Management needs more information for internal decisions and for successfully running the organization. In managing an organization the managers have to make decisions, some decisions are routine and other decision are complex.

Database is a shared corporate resource. When data is small data management is easy but data management is very difficult when database size is very large. In such cases DBMSs are inevitable for efficient and effective management of data in any organization. Irrespective of type and also sometimes size of an organization, the role of DBMS is mandatory to support correct managerial decision making at all levels in the organization while preserving data privacy, database security and integrity at all times including the database operations such as insert, update, delete, and retrieval of data.

Almost all organizations are getting potential benefits by using DBMSs. DBMS provides many facilities such as:

- Raw data are processed conveniently for obtaining desired information in many ways and in many formats such as – tables, bar charts, pie charts, graphs, diagrams etc.

- Distribution of relevant and accurate data and information to the right people at the right time.

- Reduced and controllable data redundancy makes the organization more productive and attractive for many customers.

- Speeding up all operations in the organization in a systematic way.

- Providing data security and integrity at various levels of the organization.

- Tools for three organization levels viz., top, middle, and operational levels of the organization for decision making.

A DBMS is a tool for managing data and it must be used effectively to produce the desired results. Definitely DBMS has created powerful impact in almost all organizations. DBMS–generated information has changed the way the organization functions.

Organization's management structure is divided into three levels – top, middle, and operational for ease of management. Top–level management is responsible for strategic decision making, middle level management is responsible for tactical decisions, and operational management is responsible for making operational decisions. Operational decisions are called short term decisions such as daily operations. Tactical decisions are somewhat longer than operational decisions and strategic decisions are long term decisions of an organization.

Various activities supported by DBMS at different management levels are given below:

1. Provide the information necessary for strategic decision making, strategic planning, policy formulation, and goals definition.

2. Provide access to external and internal data to identify growth opportunities and to chart the direction of such growth. Direction refers to the nature of the operations: Will a company become a service organization, a manufacturing organization, or some combination of the two?

3. Provide a framework for defining and enforcing organizational policies. Remember that such policies are translated into business rules at lower levels in the organization.

4. Improve the likelihood of a positive return on the investment for the company by searching for new ways to reduce costs and / or by boosting productivity.

5. Provide feedback to monitor whether the company is achieving its goals.

At the middle management level, the database must be able to:

1. Deliver the data necessary for tactical and planning.

2. Monitor and control the allocation and use of company resources and evaluate the performance of the various departments.

3. Provide a framework for enforcing and ensuring the security and privacy of the data in the database. Security means protecting the data against accidental or intentional use by unauthorized users. Privacy deals with the right of individuals and the organization to determine the "who, what, when, where, and how" of data usage.

At the operational management level, the database must be able to:

1. Represent and support the company operations as closely as possible. The data model must be flexible enough to incorporate all required present and expected data.

2. Provide query results within specified performance levels. Keep in mind that the performance requirements increase for lower levels of management and operations. Thus, the database must support fast responses to a greater number of transactions at the operational management level.

3. Enhance the company's short-term operational ability by providing timely information for customer support and for application development and computer operations.

3.2 Strategic Database Planning

Information systems planning are based on information engineering. Information systems planning are the starting point of database development projects. Database projects are developed to meet the diversified goals for efficient and effective data management to meet the needs and goals of organization.

Information engineering (IE) allows for the translation of the company's strategic goals into the data and applications that will help the company to achieve those goals. IE mainly concentrates on corporate data. The output of an IE is information system architecture (ISA) that works as the main basis for strategic database planning, development, and control of future information systems in the company. Information engineering methodologies are implemented using strategic planning, a commitment of resources, various managerial skills, well-defined objectives, well-defined principles, identification of critical factors, and proper management control.

Various needs of an organization are

- Improving sales,
- Providing better services to customers,
- Product quality improvement,

- Better inventory management etc.

Many database projects arise in bottom–up fashion. Database projects are requested by information system users, information system managers, developers, top management, middle management etc. Ultimately all these requirements are to improve data management in the organization. Each database project generally focuses on one particular database.

Database systems planning

The goal of database planning is to improve the business strategies of the organization with effective data management.

- Identify strategic database planning factors

Strategic database planning factors are – organization goals, critical success factors, data quality improvements, data sharing, data integration, data security, data concurrency control etc. All these factors are needed to develop useful and convenient database systems for the organization.

Identify database planning objects

Various database objects must be considered, analyzed, modified, redesigned, corrected. All business functions of the organization are identified various entity sets of the database projects in the organization are identified.

- Various database application are considered and analyzed
- Database allow data to be shared among different database application

During database planning database analysts review currently existing databases and information systems, analyze the nature of the business area with respect to the database development projects, and describe in very general terms, the data needed for each information and database system under consideration for development. Database analysts determine and verify which data are already available in existing databases and what new data will need to be added to support the proposed new projects. Out of all the database projects only important, urgent and the most necessary database projects are passed to the next phase of the database design.

Data must be viewed as a corporate resource and other corporate resources must be devoted to the development, implement and use of one or more databases. Database planning is strategic corporate effort to determine the information needs of the organization form extended period into the future. A successful database planning project will precede operational project to design, develop and implement new databases to satisfy the organizational information needs.

The need for database planning: Database planning is directed by the information needs of the organization which in turn or determined by the company's **business plan**.

Business Plan –>Information Needs–>Database Plan–>Database Development Projects.

Suppose the organization formulates its strategic business plan for the next five years. Accomplishing the objectives of this plan depends on the availability of certain identified types of information. The information can be obtained only if the data sources are identified in the database planning, or in place. This indicates the needs of the database development projects which create new database or enhance or integrate existing databases.

Database planning has significant advantages. Several advantages of formal information resource plan.

1. It expresses management current understanding of the information resources.
2. It identifies and justifies resources requirements, helping ensure that the resources will be available.
3. It identifies and justifies for effective resources management including the collaboration among departments or diligence within the organization.
4. It Specifies action plans for achieving objectives.
5. It can provide a powerful stimulus and sense of direction to employees at all levels.

Focusing these effects increasing their productivity and making them feel that they are a genuine part of the organization/ enterprise.

Envisioning change

Change is inevitable. Implementation of an effective data management strategy across the enterprise enables the organization to adapt quickly in the dynamic world of business. The ability to adapt and respond to evolving business needs, or even predict those changes in advance, will be the differentiator that allows a company to thrive. A consistent view of data throughout the enterprise is the key to be able to make informed, actionable decisions that support the vision and business strategy.

A well-thought-out data management architecture can help you take advantage of any number of opportunities that change presents. Shifts in organizational leadership, mergers and acquisitions, evolving marketing tactics and dynamic regulatory requirements can all be accommodated. Data-driven processes help you make decisions with confidence, and an enterprise data warehouse (EDW) architecture provides the ecosystem that will serve your new data management processes while accommodating future needs. The EDW also easily supports strategic operational decisions.

To aid your strategic decision making and properly direct your data management vision, you must consider what current resources are required to support your vast collection of data stores, data marts and databases, and how much value you are deriving from them. Any strategic analysis of data management possibilities would be incomplete without considering meaningful data consolidation into an EDW. For example:

- How would a single view of the business solve current challenges and deliver competitive advantages?
- How much time and effort go into reconciling numbers and validating data accuracy?
- Would greater accuracy, insights and confidence in data increase the use of decision-support and analytical tools?
- How much redundancy and inefficiency (perhaps as a result of redundant licensing, recurring infrastructure investment or administration expense) can be eliminated via consolidation?
- How would a single source for analysis and report generation mitigate business risks and support compliance initiatives?

Data processing techniques, processing power and enterprise performance management capabilities have undergone revolutionary advances in recent years.

Organizations benefit greatly from timely access to fresh data about sales, inventory movement, promotions and customers. Moving from monthly refreshes to weekly, daily, hourly or even more frequently can provide substantial incremental value.

An active data warehouse makes such timely availability a reality. In an active environment, it is possible to update information and provide intelligence throughout the organization. Corporate decision making and agility improves with new data sources, the constant inflow of fresh data and the ability of the right people to have access. Additionally, fresher data powers applications such as dashboards that provide at-a-glance status or alerts to the people who can take appropriate action on them.

Information time-sensitivity is often dependent on its type and purpose. Reports, for example, may need to be run only once a week, while certain customer or business information may be needed in real time to make operational decisions. Once your organization understands the value of its data assets, it is a matter of determining how those assets can support the corporate vision, who can best benefit from the data, when they need it and where to acquire it.

Your data, my data and our data

The days of IT telling business units what they need are long gone. Line-of-business leaders must be active in the data strategy discussions. Do not be surprised when territorial issues arise. After all, the value of corporate data is surpassed only by the territorial instincts of its departmental owners.

To address these potential challenges, it is important to work as a team and brainstorm without blinders. The discovery process is no time to be territorial, fear change or lose sight of the big picture. Nothing stifles innovation more quickly than "We've never done things that way before."

Existing processes have constraints. A major part of your discovery process should involve determining which operational processes can be automated - or even totally re-engineered - by giving access to new data resources or by linking existing data sources in new ways.

Goodbye, packaged applications; hello, innovation

Companies have more data sources than ever before. Those that effectively align their data strategies with their corporate vision are in a good position to offer innovation that can differentiate the organization from its competitors. Increasingly, gaining real competitive advantage requires unique data-driven processes and capabilities. After all, standardizing on the same data and applications as your competitors does little to help you pull away from them. According to some expert Research analysts "We are seeing a shift from packaged applications to custom capabilities that use data in new ways."

In the process, new technology must be piloted—not just to ensure performance and reliability but also to determine risks and rewards before moving on to the next phase. Because line-of-business owners are now the gatekeepers who evaluate each phase, it is essential to have them clearly define success criteria for each gate before development.

This technology evolution and innovation requires fundamental changes in the way IT develops the data management infrastructure to leverage data assets. It has also changed the role line-of-business leaders play in the process.

Today, risk can no longer be controlled through straight program management. In the past, IT primarily focused on meeting timelines and budgets while implementing technology. Now, it's more of a phase-gate process that goes far beyond implementation. Innovation creation is broken into a series of sequential phases, with gates that must be cleared before advancing to the next phase."

Creating your strategy for optimizing data management begins with understanding the role effective data management can play in achieving the overall vision for a business. Technology initiatives that affect other business units often fail when they are driven from inside IT. Executives must be on board from the start and involved in a planning process that includes all key business units. If finance, marketing, sales, production, purchasing, shipping and human resources all have input regarding what they would do with better data and what the business benefits would be, everyone will understand the grounds for prioritizing objectives, estimating return on investment and setting hard targets.

Once executive leadership understands what is possible and the business value of your data strategy, it is essential to sell the vision and drive it forward through a collaborative process that includes key business constituents. It is also important to establish realistic criteria to measure success and timelines to achieve this value.

Effective strategies are best viewed as a development continuum that is continually refined. You should revisit your data strategy at least once a year. "Best-in-class companies are measuring progress and fine-tuning their data management strategies quarterly."

Whether you're simply focusing your data management strategy or considering major direction change for the corporate vision, be sure to look to the business unit experts–it's the best way to see the whole target and aim for meaningful, continuous results.

It is a fact that database systems are becoming more complex with ever-increasing demands.

Requirements for new functionality and services, timely delivery of information, 24x7 availability, 100% integrity place enormous demands on database development projects and the teams who administer and support the environments.

Businesses must continually innovate and accept challenges. One of the certainties in life is that things will change. This is especially true of database systems that must evolve and change in response to new user requirements and the continuous drive for competitive advantage. Changes to a database may be required for bug-fixing, resolution of defects and performance tuning e.g. de-normalisation. The complexity of some systems can be overwhelming when you consider:

This is the essence of database change management. Every database development project must have a process or methodology in place to propagate and deploy upgrades to database schema and data. After all, the database is an extremely valuable asset, containing transactional, financial and customer information that are the lifeblood of an organisation.

3.3 Database and Management Control

Most important regular database management control activities are:

- Preventive management (database backup)
- Corrective management (recovery)
- Adaptive management (adding attributes, entities enhancing performance)
- Giving and revoking database access permission for new and old database users

DBMS performs many important management functions such as:

1. Data dictionary management
2. Data storages management
3. Data transformation and presentation management
4. Data security management
5. Multiuser access control management (concurrency control)

6. Backup and recovery management

7. Data integrity management

8. Database access language management

9. Application programming interfaces management

10. Database communication interfaces managements

Data dictionary management – the DBMS stores data definitions and their relationships in a data dictionary.

The database administrator (DBA) is responsible to perform routine database management activities. Proper database management is needed when data belonging to new requirements are added to the database. Sometimes, additional reports are generated and new query formats are created.

Database design and documentation should be flexible enough to implement all the changes. As the number of database applications increases, database management becomes a complex job. Database management involves upgrading the DBMS and utility software when required. Protecting the data in the database is a function of authorization management. Authorization management defines procedures to protect and guarantee database security and integrity. Some of the procedures are given below:

- User access management
    o Assigning passwords to each user
    o Define user groups
    o Assign access privileges
    o Control physical access
- View definition
- DBMS access control and
- DBMS usages monitoring

Most important aspect of managing a database is monitoring the database objects that were created in the database. A database object is basically any object created by end users. Examples for database objects are – tables, views, indexes, stored procedures, and triggers. Graphical user interfaces are also available to create, edit, view, and delete database objects.

- One of the most common database administration activities is creating and managing database users.

- Fine-tuning a database is another important DBA task.

- Management of data storage media for database backups is based on database accessibility, database cost and database security

Efficient data management typically requires the use of a computer database. DBMS software manages the database within the database system. Database systems can be created and managed at different levels of complexity.

3.4 The Information Domain

1. An information system is designed to process data, i.e. to accept input data, manipulate it in some way, and produce output called information.

2. It is also designed to process events – an event represents a problem or system control which triggers data processing procedures in an information system.

3. The information domain of an information system therefore includes both data (i.e. characters, numbers, images and sound) and events (i.e. problem and control)

The process of identifying information contents and relationships is known as data modeling in information system design.

1. information flow – the ways by which data and events change as they are processed by the information system

2. the process of identifying information flow is known as process modeling in information system design

Information organization and data structure (data model) are not only important for the management of data, but also for the development of software applications that utilize these data

3.4.1 The data-oriented approach to information systems

An information system contains four components: data, technology, process (or application) and people. Information systems are designed and developed to process, manage and analyze data in support of the business objectives of an organization. Of the four components of information systems, data are most stable but data are most expensive to acquire.

Managing data as a valuable corporate resource in the same way financial, technical and human resources are managed. This is the basis of the concept of information resource management (IRM)

- Sharing data among different users or user groups help maximize the cost-benefit ratio of the capital investments on information systems. Specifications of hardware and software must be able to meet data requirements, but not to change data requirements in order to suit the characteristics or functionality of hardware and software

- Data-driven application development
  - software applications are designed to enable the effective and efficient use of data in business operation and decision making
  - information systems are used in organizations as an opportunity to re-engineer business, i.e. to change the philosophy and ways of running a business
  - ensuring that information organization meets the business needs of an organization is the responsibility of a small team of technical staff under the leadership of a database administrator
  - system developers design and build software applications, however, system developers may also assist in defining information organization by taking part in user requirement studies

  Many projects fail because of the lack of understanding of information management but not because of the lack of capability of technology. Identification of users' requirements, which forms the foundation of good design and correct specification of information management, is always the most important step in information system development. The ultimate goal of information management is to create the necessary technical environment that allows the development of information systems which are:

  - cost-effective to implement – by the ability to use shared data and possibly applications by users in different organizations
  - flexible to build – by permitting the addition or removal of applications, in response to changing needs and objectives of the information users, without affecting existing data structure
  - easy to use – by eliminating the need of the regular users to worry about the structure of the data

Information management
- information management can be understood from four perspectives:

56

- o   a data perspective
- o   a relationship perspective
- o   an operating system (OS) perspective
- o   an application architecture perspective

3.4.2   The data perspective of information management

- data must be considered in terms of descriptive elements and graphical elements because
  - o   these two types of data elements have distinctly different characteristics
  - o   they have different storage requirements
  - o   they have different processing requirements

For descriptive data, the most basic element of information organization is called a data item. A data item represents an occurrence or instance of a particular characteristic pertaining to an entity (which can be a person, thing, event or phenomenon). It is the smallest unit of stored data in a database, commonly referred to as an attribute. In database terminology, an attribute is also referred to as a stored field. The value of an attribute can be in the form of a number (integer or floating-point), a character string, a date or a logical expression (e.g. T for 'true' or 'present"; F for 'false' or 'absent')

A group of related data items form a record. In database terminology, a record is always formally referred to as a stored record. A set of related records constitutes a data file. A data file is individually identified by a filename. The concept of database is the approach to information management in computer-based data processing today. A database is defined as an automated, formally defined and centrally controlled collection of persistent data used and shared by different users in an enterprise. "centrally controlled" does not mean "physically centralized" --- databases today tend to be physically distributed in different computer systems, at the same or different locations

A database is set up to serve the information needs of an organization. Data sharing is key to the concept of database. Data in a database are described as "permanent" in the sense that they are different from "transient" data such as input to and output from an information system. The data usually remain in the database for a considerable length of time, although the actual content of the data can change very frequently.

Data in a database are still organized and stored as data files. The use of database represents a change in the perception of data, the mode of data processing and the purposes of using the data, rather than physical storage of the data. Databases can be organized in different ways known as database models. Three conventional database models are: relational, network and hierarchical

- relational – data are organized by records in relations which resemble a table
- network – data are organized by records which are classified into record types, with m:n pointers linking associated records
- hierarchical – data are organized by records on a parent-child one-to-many relations

The emerging database model is object-oriented

- data are uniquely identified as individual objects that are classified into object types or classes according to the characteristics (attributes and operations) of the object

3.4.3 The relationship perspective of information organization

Relationships represent an important concept in information organization – it describes the logical association between entities. Relationships can be categorical or spatial, depending on whether they describe location or other characteristics

The operating system (OS) perspective of information organization

From the operating system perspective, information is organized in the form of directories. Directories are a special type of computer files used to organize other files into a hierarchical structure. Directories are also referred to as folders, particularly in systems using graphical user interfaces. A directory may also contain one of more directories

The application architecture perspective of information management

Computer applications nowadays tend to be constructed on the client/server systems architecture. client/server is primarily a relationship between processes running in the same computer or, more commonly, in separate computers across a telecommunication network

- o the client is a process that requests services
    - the dialog between the client and the server is always initiated by the client

- a client can request services from many servers at the same time
  - the server is a process that provides the service
    - a server is primarily a passive service provider
    - a server can service many clients at the same time
- there are many ways of implementing a client/server architecture but from the perspective of information management, the following five are most important
  - file servers – the client requests specific records from a file; and the server returns these records to the client by transmitting them across the network
  - database servers – the client sends structured query language (SQL) requests to the server; the server finds the required information by processing these requests and then passes the results back to the client
  - transaction servers – the client invokes a remote procedure that executes a transaction at the server side; the server returns the result back to the client via the network
  - Web server – communicating interactively by the Hypertext Transfer Protocol (HTTP) over the Internet, the Web server returns documents when clients ask for them by name
  - groupware servers – this particular type of servers provides a set of applications that allow clients (and their users) to communicate with one another using text, images, bulletin boards, video and other forms of media
- from the application architecture perspective, the objective of information management is to develop a data design strategy that will optimize system operation by
  - balancing the distribution of data resources between the client and the server
    - databases are typically located on the server to enable data sharing by multiple users
    - data that are commonly used together should be placed in the same server

- data that have common security requirements should be placed in the same server

- data intended for a particular purpose (file service, database query, transaction processing, Web browsing or groupware applications) should be placed in the appropriate server

  o standardizing and maintaining metadata (i.e. data about data) to facilitate the search for the availability and characteristics of existing data

3.4.4 Data Structure

As most commercial implementations of information systems today are based on the relational and object-oriented database models

3.5 Risks and Costs of Database Management Systems (DBMSs)

A significant disadvantage of the DBMS is its cost.

3.5.1 New specialized personnel

People with special skills are needed to obtain potential benefits. Special skills are needed

1. To design, develop and implement databases
2. To provide database administration (DBA) services or functions
3. To manage personnel and to train people

3.5.2 Installation and management cost and complexity

Database systems are usually very large. Installation and setup costs are very high. Costs for training, data communication, software up gradation, software maintenance, support etc are very high.

3.5.3 Conversion costs

Old application software system must be converted into new application software system. Extra money, time, commitment and personnel required.

3.5.4 Need for explicit backup and recovery

Database systems are very large and data is most important and valuable resource. So, explicit, backup is needed and special database recovery techniques are also needed.

3.5.5 Organization conflicts

Database is a shared resource. Hence there should not be any conflicts on data definitions, data formats, coding and ownership for control and accurate data maintenance

3.5.6 New Hardware and Software costs

3.6 Self Assessment Questions

3.6.1 Short Answer Questions

1. What is the relation between information systems and organizations?

2. What are the main points in strategic database planning?

3.6.2 Essay Questions

1. Explain about database systems in the organization.

2. Explain the need of strategic database planning.

3. Explain about database and management control.

4. Explain about information domain.

5. Explain about risks and costs of database management systems (DBMSs)

CHAPTER 4
DATABASE DEVELOPMENT

Objectives

- ✓ To know about database development
- ✓ To understand database development methodologies
- ✓ To study the classification of DBMSs
- ✓ To know when is DBMS inappropriate
- ✓ To study the characteristics of database approach
- ✓ To understand the goals of DBMS

Chapter Structure

4.1 Introduction

4.2 Database Development under the Control of the Information Systems

4.3 Database Development

4.4 Classification of Database Management Systems

4.5 Core database Technology Trend

4.6 When is DBMS Inappropriate?

4.7 The main characteristics of the database approach

4.8 The goals of a Database Management System

4.9 Self Assessment Questions

4.1 Introduction

Database is one part of information system. Database development process should fit into the overall information systems development process. Database development activities should coordinate with all the other activities in the development of a complete information system.

4.2 Database Development under the Control of the Information Systems

In several organizations, database development begins with corporate (Enterprise) data modeling. Enterprise data modeling is the first step in database development. Enterprise data modeling sets scope, general ideas, general data contents, describes the scope of data maintained by the organization, range of databases, database needs, types of users, number of users in the organization, size and complexity of databases, and general requirements of the organization etc. Database development process occurs during information systems planning for an organization. The purpose of enterprise data modeling is to create or produce an overall or general idea or general details of an organizational database. Enterprise data modeling concentrates only on general data details of the organization but not database design details.

Enterprise data modeling consists of many databases and many information systems. Each database supports for one or more information systems. During enterprise data modeling database development personnel or staff analyses currently existing information systems and databases, analyze the nature of the business areas to be supported, required data details and operations are specified at a very high level of abstraction, and plans are initiated for one or more database projects.

Enterprise data modeling is specified in a very high level data model called conceptual data model. There exist many conceptual data models – Entity Relationship (ER) data model, Enhanced Entity Relationship (EER) data model, Unified Markup Language (UML) data model etc.

4.2.1 Information Systems Architecture (ISA)

Information system architecture encompasses several components. An enterprise data model is one important component or part of the overall information system architecture. ISA shows or expresses high level plans for all the information systems in the organization. Enterprise data model (EDM) is developed as a part of total information systems architecture or overall organization plan for the data resources. ISA consists of six main components:

Data	Data are collection of values or facts or raw values.
Processes	A process accepts input data, processes input data in a specified manner, and produces results called outputs.
Networks	A network is a collection of connected components in a specified manner. Network transmits data between and among the various components.
People	People perform or execute processes and people are the main sources and receivers of data.
Events and points in time	Events occur when processes are performed.
Reasons	Data are processed based on rules and events are occurred after processing

Definitely we need a high level approach for the development of information systems as well as development of database systems in organizations. A very high level data management should be needed because of the following reasons:

1. We cannot develop an information system or a database system without a plan.

2. As time goes on changes are inevitable in the database. It is very difficult to apply changes in the database without a plan. A plan anticipates changes in the database.

3. Without a high level data model it is very difficult to develop database systems or information systems.

With high level data model such as enterprise data modeling it is very easy to develop database systems because we know about the data details, user details, information needs, data requirements, inputs and outputs etc. Also enterprise data modeling allows data architecture reusability. Reusability decreases many problems, development time, complexity of many database projects.

4.2.2 Information Engineering (IE)

Information management systems architecture is developed by information systems planners by using a well defined and a particular methodology for information systems planning. Information engineering (IE) is one of the most popular methodologies for developing an architectural planning of information system. IE is a top-down methodology and it uses a data orientation approach to create and maintain information systems in the organizations. IE mainly concentrates only in understanding the relevant data details that are needed to develop information systems.

In information engineering enterprise data are modeled in a very high level but not in a very too much detail. Information engineering is independent of technology and data usage. It first analyses broadly very high level details of an organization and then creates more specific information systems to meet the needs at various levels of the organization from top to bottom. Information engineering allows what information systems are needed at low level of an organization? How information systems are developed to meet the objectives of various parts of the organization? It allows easy understanding of the relationships between information systems and business objectives and goals.

Information engineering contains four main steps or phases:

1. Planning
2. Analysis
3. Design and
4. Implementation

Planning

Planning phase of information engineering produces very high level components of an information system architecture (ISA) such as enterprise data modeling (EDM). The main goal of information system planning phase is to support information technology with various business strategies of the organization in order to obtain maximum benefits from investments in information systems and technologies.

The steps in the planning phase of the information engineering are given below:

1. Identify strategic planning factors
   a. Goals
   b. Critical success factors
   c. Problem areas
2. Identify corporate planning objects
   a. Organizational units
   b. Locations
   c. Business functions
   d. Entity sets
3. Develop an enterprise data model
   a. Functional decomposition
   b. Entity Relationship Diagram (ERD)
   c. Planning matrices

The purpose of **identifying strategic planning** factors is to develop the planning context and to link information systems plans to the strategic business functions. These strategic planning factors help information system managers to set priorities among the many information systems, create requests for starting new information systems, and initiate some database development projects in a planned way.

Corporate planning objects must be identified. The corporate planning objects define the business scope. The business scope limits and restricts the further systems analysis and it allows us to find where the information system changes are needed and where changes are not needed. Some of the important corporate planning objects are:

1. Organizational units
2. Organizational locations
3. Business functions
4. Entity types and
5. Information systems

An enterprise data model is developed. An enterprise data model consists of three main components–functional decomposition models of each business function, an enterprise data model, and planning matrices. Functional breakdown method follows from top to bottom and divides the main business functions into smaller and with greater details. An enterprise data model is often represented using entity relationship diagram (ERD). An ERD shows not only the entity sets but also shows the relationships among the entities. Other relationships, between various business planning objects are also represented by using enterprise data modeling. Planning matrices are useful for setting development priorities, sequencing development activities, and scheduling those activities from top-to-bottom

4.3 Database Development

Planning of information systems is based on information engineering. Information systems planning is one main source of developing new database projects to meet the strategic and dynamic needs of the organization. There may be many organizational needs such as

- Improving quality of services
- Reducing the product price
- Improving the sales of products
- Improving inventory management
- Better and accurate sales forecasting etc.
- Reducing the waiting times of customers
- Improving the quality of the products
- Improving the business standards

The proposals for starting new information systems and then for new database systems may come from any location in the organization including from bottom up

66

passion also. In general information systems are needed to perform new tasks in an easy way or to improve the existing methods of doing tasks. Thorough analysis must be carried out when proposals for information systems exist. Analyze and check whether existing systems can provide necessary functions. If not, then find what new database systems are needed.

Normally each database system development project focuses on one particular database. Different database projects may be in different phases of development. In many cases database systems and related processing functions together are developed as part of the information system development in many organizations.

System Development Life Cycle (SDLC)

SDLC is a method of systematically developing information systems. Information system professionals including system analysts, database designers, database developers, and programmers follow SDLC steps. SDLC consists of steps as shown below:

1. Planning
2. Analysis
3. Design
4. Development
5. Testing
6. Implementation
7. Maintenance

Planning

All the user requirements and requested proposals are collected, priorities are assigned, written requests are prepared to study the currently existing systems or to start developing of new systems for providing solutions to some problems. Requested proposals contain problems and possible solutions to the problems.

Analysis

Thorough analysis of the corresponding requested proposals is performed. After thorough analysis requirements are determined, listed and structured in documents such as systems requirements specification (SRS). If the list contains many more requirements the potential requirements are selected. Functional specifications which are feasible and implementable are prepared to meet the user requirements.

Design

Detailed functional specifications of all data, forms, reports, results, calculations, inputs, outputs, required technology, program structures, database structures, file designs, record designs, index details, physical sites, organizational redesigns etc are specified without any ambiguity.

Development

Required software is developed according to the specifications to satisfy the needs of the users in the organization.

Testing

First data is loaded into the database and database tests are performed for database integrity, security, performance, adjustments, fine tuning, concurrent data access etc.

Implementation

Database application programs are developed, tested, and installed. Necessary documentation is prepared, users are given training. Data is loaded from existing files to new database files. Finally database and database application programs are put into correctly for production purpose in such way that data is properly maintaining and database users are storing and retrieving data correctly.

Maintenance

Errors are detected and corrected. Different types of maintenances such as corrective maintenance, adaptive maintenance, enhancement etc are applied. All operations are monitored and strengths and weaknesses of the information system are identified.

Steps in database development

Database development also contains steps similar to SDLC but always there is no one-to-one correspondence between SDLC steps and database development steps.

Planning

Database analysts study and review already existing database projects and data scope is specified. Also they reveal that what are the new database projects that are needed for new information systems. They determine what are the data already exists and what new data items are needed etc. potential database projects are put in priority queue. A high level conceptual data model called an enterprise data model is constructed. Only entities and the relationships among entities are specified. Constraints on the data values are also specified. Also necessary documentation is prepared.

Analysis

A detailed data model of the organizational data is prepared. This data is supposed to use in information systems. All attributes, data type of attributes, integrity constrains on data are clearly specified and modified according to needs of the organization. In detailed conceptual data model is the output of this analysis phase. This detailed model is also checked for consistency with other data models such as EER, UML etc.

Logical Database Design

High level conceptual data model is transformed into selected DBMS model. In most of the cases relational model is the logical data model. Detailed reviews are performed including inputs, outputs, reports, forms, data entry procedures, displays, transactions etc. The database analysts pinpoint and verify exactly what data are to be manipulated, managed and supported in the database. Sometimes it may be necessary to modify the details with respect to transactions, reports, forms etc. Additional information processing requirements and database requirements are also added to the system. Finally, modified logical database design is transformed into one which is well structured, well organized, and easy to understand specifications without any ambiguities.

Physical Database Design

Points to be considered in this phase are

1. Selecting the best file organization
2. Creating the indexes for performance improvement
3. Well designing record formats.
4. Implementing logical relationships
5. Converting logical data structures into physical structures
6. Specifying data type, data length for each attribute
7. Creating primary key for each relation

Database implementation

Database application programs are developed, tested, and installed. Necessary documentation is prepared, users are given training, and all procedures and policies are placed in right place to follow. Data is loaded from existing files to new database files. Finally database and database application programs are put into correctly for production purpose in such way that data is properly maintaining and database users are storing and retrieving data correctly.

Database Maintenance

Database changes as time changes. During database maintenance data are inserted, modified, deleted, and selected as needed. Dynamically errors are corrected and structures are added, modified, deleted for improving the database performance. Structure and data are modified as needed to meet the changing business conditions. Database must be rebuilt when database is damaged. Periodically database backups are taken. Constraints are added, indexes are added, modified, and deleted whenever necessary for database system performance improvement.

4.4 Classification of Database Management Systems (DBMSs)

Database management systems (DBMSs) are classified based on

1. Data model
2. Number of users
3. Number of sites or locations
4. Cost of the DBMS
5. Expected type and extent of use

4.4.1 Data model

Classification of DBMSs based on data model are – Relational DBMSs (RDBMSs), Object DBMSs (ODBMSs), Object-relational DBMSs (ORDBMSs), Hierarchical DBMSs (HDBMSs), Network DBMSs (NDBMS).

4.4.2 Number of users

DBMSs used in personal computers are called single user database management systems. Multiuser DBMSs allow using the same database by many users concurrently.

4.4.3 Number of sites or locations

In centralized DBMSs total database is stored in one single computer. In distributed database management systems (DDBMSs) database and DBMS software are stored in many locations. In homogeneous DDBMSs all locations have the same DBMS software where as in non homogeneous DDBMSs different DBMSs softwares exist at different locations or sites.

4.4.4 Cost based classification of DBMSs

DBMS such as MS Access is available for low cost where as ORACLE is available for high cost. Some DBMSs are general purpose and other DBMSs are special purpose.

In general database systems are classified as follows:

1. Single-user database supports only one user at a time

    Desktop database – single-user, runs on PC

2. Multiuser database supports multiple users at the same time

    Workgroup database supports a small number

    Enterprise database supports a large number

3. Centralized database – data located at a single site

4. Distributed database – data distributed across several different sites

5. Operational database – supports a company's day-to-day operations

    Transactional or production database

6. Data warehouse – stores data used for tactical or strategic decisions

7. Unstructured data exist in their original state. Semi-structured data have been processed to some extent. XML database supports semi-structured XML data. Extensible Markup Language (XML) represents data elements in textual format

4.5 Core database Technology Trend

1. Relational Database
2. Distributed Database
3. Multi-dimensional databases
4. Object-Oriented Database
5. Object Relational Database
6. Multimedia Database
7. Intelligent Database
8. Data warehousing, data marts, data mining
9. Web-based Databases

4.6 When is DBMS Inappropriate?

1. Database is small and has simple structure
2. Applications are simple and special-purpose
3. Applications with real-time requirements

71

4. Concurrent, multi-user access to data is not needed

4.7 The main characteristics of the database approach

1. Self-describing nature of a database system
2. Insulation between programs and data, and data abstraction.
3. Support of multiple views of the data.
4. Sharing of data and multiuser transaction processing.

4.7.1 Self-describing nature of a database system:

A fundamental characteristic of the database approach is that the database system contains not only the database itself but also a complete definition or description of the database structure and constraints. The definition is stored in the DBMS catalog, which contain information such as the structure of each file, the type and storage format of each data item, and various constraints on the data. The information stored in the catalog is called metadata, which describes the structure of the primary database.

4.7.2 Insulation between programs and data, and data abstraction

A data model is used to hide storage details and present the users with a conceptual view of the database. Insulation between programs and data is called data independence.

4.7.3 Support of multiple views of the data

Each user may see a different view of the database, which describes only the data of interest to that user. Different parts of the data are given to different users of the database.

4.7.4 Sharing of data and multi-user transaction processing

4.8 The goals of a Database Management System

The goals of a Database Management System can be summarized as follows:

1. Data storage, retrieval, and update (while hiding the internal physical implementation details)
2. A user-accessible catalog
3. Transaction support
4. Concurrency control services (multi-user update functionality)
5. Recovery services (damaged database must be returned to a consistent state)
6. Authorization services (security)
7. Support for data communication Integrity services (i.e. constraints)

72

8. Services to promote data independence

9. Utility services (i.e. importing, monitoring, performance, record deletion, etc.)

The components to facilitate the goals of a DBMS may include the following:

1. Query processor

2. Data Manipulation Language preprocessor

3. Database manager (software components to include authorization control, command processor, integrity checker, query optimizer, transaction manager, scheduler, recovery manager, and buffer manager)

4. Data Definition Language compiler

5. File manager

6. Catalog manager

4.9. Self Assessment Questions

4.9.1 Short Answer Questions

1. What is information systems architecture (ISA)?

2. What is information engineering (IE)?

3. What is the core database technology trend?

4. When is DBMS Inappropriate?

4.9.2 Essay Questions

1. Explain database development under the control of the information systems.

2. Explain about database development.

3. How database management systems are classified?

4. What are the main characteristics of the database approach?

5. What are the goals of a database management system?

CHAPTER 5

DATABASE DESIGN

Objectives

- ✓ To know about database design
- ✓ To understand the steps in database design

Chapter Structure

5.1   Introduction

5.2   Database Design

5.3   Data Modeling / Database Design

5.4   Steps in Database Design

5.5   Self assessment questions

5.1 Introduction

Database design is a corner stone for developing good and effective databases in organizations. For effective decision making we need accurate and timely data stored in the databases. Well organized data is available only when databases are designed and developed in a systematic way. Hence, databases are developed by using a sequence of well formulated steps.

5.2 Database Design

Database design is the process of producing a detailed data model of a database. The term database design can be used to describe many different parts of the design of an overall database system. The conceptual data model is mapped to a logical data model, such as the relational model; this in turn is mapped to a physical model during physical design.

5.3 Data Modeling / Database Design

Database Design

Database design is the activity of specifying the schema of a database in a given data model.

Database Schema

Database schema is the structure of a database that captures data types, relationships, constraints on the data. Database schema is independent of any application program. Database schema changes infrequently.

Database instance or database state

The actual data stored in the database at a given time is called database instance.

Data Model

A set of primitives for defining the logical structure of a database and a set of operations for specifying the insert, update, delete and retrievals on a database. Examples for data models are – relational, hierarchical, network, object-oriented, object-relational.

5.4 Steps in Database Design

The process of database design is divided into different steps. They are

1. Requirement Analysis
2. Conceptual Database Design (ER-Diagram)
3. Logical Database Design (Tables, Normalization etc)
4. Schema Refinement
5. Physical Database Design (Table Indexing, Clustering etc)
6. Database System Implementation and Tuning
7. Database Maintenance

5.4.1 Requirements analysis

In this phase a detailed analysis of the requirements is performed. The objective of this phase is to get a clear understanding of the requirements. It makes use of various information gathering methods for this purpose. Some of them are

- Interview
- Analyzing existing documents
- Survey
- Site visit
- Joint Applications Design (JAD) and Joint Requirements Analysis (JRA)

Requirements analysis is the first step in database design. This step is crucial to the success of the information system. The scope and general contents of organizational databases are specified. Overall data details of an organization are provided at a very high level of abstraction. The overall data requirements of the database are analyzed. Data requirements are collected with respect to database usage, database application, types of users (new and old). What are the potential operations? such as insert, modify, delete and retrieval of the database are analyzed.

Database designers have to study the existing system to identify data requirements, requirements of users, data volume, system performance requirements, security issues, data access permissions, number of users and database operations. Also identify problems of the database system and formulate standards and guidelines.

A database is designed for a particular database application. Different databases are needed for different database applications. First identify what data are to be stored in the database, what are the different database operations. You have to find what the users want from the database. Indentify and analyze user requirements. Identify most important database operations, workloads, queries etc by interacting users, customers.

Thorough study of existing documents – manuals, reports, registers, forms, bills is needed. Information flows, types of transactions, types of users, types of data operations must be analyzed. By using interviews, observation, record review, questionnaire collect full and complete data requirements of users, customers and other stake holders.

Conduct meetings and workshops for active participation of users, customers, stake holders etc. use requirements specification techniques such as data flow diagram (DFD), object oriented analysis (OOA) etc to transform requirements into a better structured form. Prepare documentation in the form of text, tables, bar charts, pie charts.

Use tools such as CASE tools to check the consistency and completeness of requirements specifications. Many tools are used to trace the links between requirements and other design entities such as code modules, test cases, change of management procedures, modification of documents etc. Database designers have to interact and interview with database users to understand data requirements of users and to document the collected data requirements of users.

After analysis, user's requirements are collected and documented. Data requirements and functional requirements are identified and documented. Totally, all the database requirements are analyzed, collected and documented in a database requirements specification document.

At the end of requirements analysis step detailed and complete lists of database requirements are documented.

An enterprise data model is often described using entity relationship diagram. Current data details and overall data requirements are analyzed. After analysis, analysts have to specify new data details that are required. The analyst produces a detailed data model that identifies all the organizational data.

5.4.2 Conceptual database design

The second step called creation of conceptual database schema begins after all the requirements have been collected, analyzed and documented in detail. This step is independent of database application and database system software and it is easy to understand, modify, add, delete, and to communicate with nontechnical users of the database. This step, conceptual database schema, ensures that all user data requirements are met without any conflicts. Only data descriptions are analyzed and documented but not implemented.

The requirement analysis is modeled in this conceptual design. The ER Model is used at the conceptual design stage of the database design. The ER diagram is used to represent this conceptual design. ER diagram consists of Entities, Attributes and Relationships.

Data requirements of database users are identified, data attributes, entities and relationships between entities are represented. Integrity rules are specified. A very high-level conceptual data model called entity-relationship (ER) data model is developed based on the information details obtained in requirements analysis steps. ER data model shows diagrammatically data relationships, data descriptions, data constraints, other details of data to be stored in the database. ER data model is an approximate description of the data. Data entities and relationships among those entities are specified.

A conceptual scheme for the database is created using a high-level conceptual data model.

Conceptual database schema is created using a high–level conceptual data model called Entity Relationship (ER) data model. Conceptual database schema contains a detailed descriptions of the data requirements of the database users, entity sets, data relationships, integrity constraints, rules etc. All these details are described or represented using a high level data model called ER data model.

A conceptual database schema that is independent of a specific DBMS is created with high level data model, ER or EER or UML data model is used to create conceptual database schema. Conceptual database schema is designed based on the data requirements obtained in requirements analysis. Conceptual database schema is specified in a very high level data model and it is independent of any DBMS.

High-level conceptual database schema design shows full details of data, database structure, data constraints, data relationships, meaning etc. it shows a stable description of the database contents. Database users, customers, application designers have to understand the conceptual database schema model thoroughly and completely. High level pictorial or diagrammatic representation or description of the conceptual database schema can serve as an excellent vehicle of communication among database designers, database users, database analysts, customers, stakeholders, database application developers.

High-level conceptual database schema design model should have features or characteristic such as expressiveness, simple and understandable, formal, general, minimal, interpretable, high-level, and independent of low level details. Strategies used for conceptual database schema design are top down, bottom up, inside out, mixed strategies.

5.4.3 Logical database design

Once the relationships and dependencies are identified the data can be arranged into logical structures and is mapped into database management system tables. Normalization is performed to make the relations in appropriate normal forms.

Logical database design is software dependent. The conceptual database design called conceptual data model or ER data model is converted into the selected data model of the DBMS. This step is called database schema preparation. Relational data model is the most popular data model. So, ER data model is converted into relational data model. Logical database design means preparing logical schema. In relational data model a database is a collection of relations. For RDBMSs, the logical database design includes the design of tables, indexes, views, transactions, access privileges and queries etc.

The result of logical database design is a database schema in the implementation data model of the selected commercial DBMS. The result of this phase should be DDL statements in the language of the selected DBMS. External schemas or views are also created. Sometimes the conceptual database schema is translated from high–level data model into the implementation data model of the selected commercial DBMS such as relational or object or object relational data model.

5.4.4 Schema Refinement

Refine or modify the relations in such a way that redundancy is reduced, insertion, modification, deletion and query operations are easy to apply.

5.4.5 Physical Database Design

The physical database design of the database specifies the physical configuration of the database on the secondary storage media. That is physical database design deals with the physical implementation of the database in a database management system (DBMS). This includes detailed specification of data elements, data types, indexing options and other parameters residing in the data dictionary. All these information are stored in the data dictionary.

In physical database design, file organizations, record designs, indexes creation, clustering of records, clustering of indexes, estimation of typical work loads, queries, storage structures and access path specification, choice of tree indexes or hash indexes etc are designed and applied.

Physical database design options are – response time, disk space utilization, execution time, data transfer rates, throughputs and performance etc.

File design, record design, and suitable physical data structure are specified. Some relations are clustered and indexes such as tree index or hash indexes are created for some relations. Record design may be fixed length record or variable length records. File design may be sequential file access or indexed file access or indexed sequential file access or direct file access or hashing file access.

Internal storage structures, file organizations for the database files, record design, creation of indexes, access paths are specified.

5.4.6 Database System Implementation and Tuning

Table spaces, data files and tables are created. Database designers write, test and install the programs that process the database. Database documentation is provided, users are trained, manuals are updated and procedures are specified for support of database, and associated database applications are put into production for data maintenance.

Database and application programs are implemented, tested, corrected, tuned and deployed for production use. Database tuning operations such as physical design changes, data indexing, data reorganization etc are performed. Database tuning is an ongoing activity.

Database schemas and empty database systems files are created. The database is loaded with data. Once the data is loaded into the database, the design and implementation phase is over and the operation phase of the database system begins.

One thing is clear that database requirements are always change continuously. So, it is necessary to add or remove or modify tables, indexes, views, and reorganize some files by changing the file access methods, adding or dropping indexes etc. Some queries or transactions may be rewritten for better database performance.

Database tuning is an ongoing process as long as there are changes in database requirements and performance problems exist in the database.

5.4.7 Database Maintenance

Database is tailored or modified to meet the needs of the changing business requirements or conditions, to correct errors in the database or to improve the processing speed of database applications. If any problem occurs the database designers must be able to construct the database and tune database for improved performance. Fix and correct errors in database.

5.5 Self Assessment Questions

5.5.1 Short Answer Questions

1. Define database design
2. Define database schema
3. What is the importance of conceptual database design?
4. What is the importance of physical database design?
5. What do you mean by database implementation?

5.5.2 Essay Questions

1. Explain database design steps in detail

CHAPTER – 6
CONCEPTUAL DATABASE DESIGN

Objectives

- ✓ To understand the principle of conceptual database design
- ✓ To study the advantages of conceptual database design
- ✓ To study about different types of conceptual database models
- ✓ To understand aggregation
- ✓ To study entity relationship (ER) data modeling

Chapter Structure

6.1   Introduction

6.2   Principles of Conceptual Database Design

6.3   Advantages of Conceptual Database Models

6.4   Conceptual Data Models

6.5   Aggregation

6.6   Entity-Relationship (ER) data model and Entity-Relationship Diagrams (ERDs)

6.7   Modeling Conceptual Objects versus Physical Objects

6.8   Entity Relationship Diagram (ERD) Example

6.9   Self Assessment Questions

6.1 Introduction

Conceptual data models are the most important data models for defining, describing, and explaining higher level details of the system or organization. These models are independent of hardware and software. They are very useful to analyze overall data requirements of the business functions of the organization. They depict detailed specification of the overall structure of organizational data. They show graphical or pictorial representation of the organizational data, data relationships, constraints etc. Conceptual data models are usually described by using entity relationship (ER) modeling or enhanced entity relationship (EER) modeling or object modeling, or unified modeling language (UML) notations.

6.2 Principles of Conceptual Database Design

Principles of conceptual database design are given below:

6.2.1 Diagrammatic Representation

The model should have a diagrammatic notation for displaying a conceptual schema that is easy to interpret and understand.

6.2.2 Hardware Independent

Hardware independence means that the model does not depend on the hardware used in the implementation of the model.

6.2.3 Software Independent

Software independence means that the model does not depend on the DBMS software used to implement the model.

6.2.4 Simplicity and Understandability

The model should be simple enough for typical non-specialist users to understand and use its concepts.

6.2.5 Comprehensibility

Easy to understand

6.2.6 Interpretability

Easy to learn, explain, and interpret

6.2.7 Extensibility

The model should be easy to extend with additional components.

6.28 Expressiveness

Conceptual data model should include expressive enough features to distinguish different types of data, entities, relationships, constraints, limitations.

6.2.9 Minimality

The model should have a small number of basic concepts that are distinct and non- overlapping in meaning.

6.2.10 Formality

A conceptual schema expressed in the data model must represent a formal unambiguous specification of the data. Hence the model concepts must be defined accurately and unambiguously.

6.3 Advantages of Conceptual Database Models

1. Conceptual database design can be implemented in any database model.
2. Conceptual database design avoids specific details of any database model.
3. It represents the real world as closely as possible.

4. Consistency and integrity principles or features or characteristics of conceptual database design allow representing real world behavior, situations and transformations very closely and accurately.

5. Conceptual database design is very easy to understand even novice users also.

6. It shows only high level details of the organization graphically.

7. It represents a global view of the entire database as viewed by the entire organization.

8. It integrates entities, relationships, constraints, and processes into a single global view of the entire data in the organization.

9. It provides a relatively easily understood macro level view of the data environment.

10. It is the basis for the identification and high-level description of the main data objects.

11. It creates an abstract database design that represents real-world objects in the most realistic way.

12. Conceptual database design represents the real world problem or event in very high level and easily understandable graphical diagram.

13. It is portable across different platforms and systems. Portability extends the life of database.

14. Database users and database designers can understand conceptual database design very easily.

15. It provides a stable description of database contents.

16. It is more expressive and general.

6.4 Conceptual Data Models

Basic components needed to construct the conceptual data model are attributes, entities, entity sets, relationships, relationship sets, primary key, foreign key, cardinality and participation constraints, weak entity sets, specialization, generalization, hierarchies, lattices etc.

Different data models have different features. Some data models are better suited than others for some tasks. For example, conceptual data models are better suited for high level data modeling, while implementation models are better for managing stored data for implementation purpose.

- Entity relationship (ER) data model is an example of a conceptual data model.

- Hierarchical and network data models are implementation models.

- Relation data model (RDM), object oriented data model (OODM) can be used as both conceptual and implementation models.

- ER data model is only conceptual data model and it is not an implementation model.

- Unified Modeling Language (UML) has been proposed as a standard for conceptual object modeling. That is, object oriented data modeling (OODM) system design is represented by using the high level conceptual data model called Unified Modeling Language (UML).

Conceptual database design is specified in many high-level data models such as

1. Entity Relationship (ER) Data Model
2. Enhanced Entity Relationship (EER) Data Model
3. Object-Oriented data Model
4. Object-Relational Data Model, and
5. Unified Markup Language (UML) etc.

6.4.1 Entity Relationship (ER) Data Model

The most famous and widely used conceptual data model is the entity relationship (ER) data model. ER data model is graphically represented by entity relationship diagram (ERD). ER data model is represented in terms of entities, the relationships among those entities, and attributes of both entities and relationships. Entity relationship data model is the most frequently used conceptual data model. Attributes that are directly connected to the relationship set are called descriptive attributes.

An ER data model is a detailed, high level logical representation of the data for an organization in terms of high level. ER data model shows only high level relationships among the elements such as attributes, entities, relationships, relationship sets etc.

Some important components or elements of an entity relationship (ER) data model are given below:

Rectangles – to represent entity sets

Ellipses – to represent attributes

Diamonds – to represent relationship sets

Double ellipses – to represent multi valued attributes

Dashed ellipses – to represent derived attributes (calculated attributes)

Double rectangles – to represent weak entity sets

Double diamonds – to represent relationship with weak entity sets (Identifying relationship)

6.4.2 Enhanced Entity Relationship (EER) Data Model

The most important modeling construct in enhanced entity relationship (EER) data model is supertype/ subtype relationship. EER is an extension of entity relationship (ER) set. First, we model a general entity set and then we model sub entities of that general entity set. General entity set is called supertype and the sub entities are called subtypes. A subtype inherits all the properties of its supertype and it can have its own additional properties and can participate in relationships of its own. EER data model is used to represent conceptual data model of the organization.

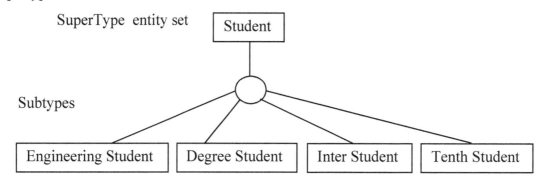

Figure 6.1 Supertype/ subtype relationship

Attribute inheritance

Every subtype is also an entity set by its own. Attribute inheritance is a property where each subtype inherits all attribute values form its supertype. Every member of a subtype must be a member of a supertype but the converse may or may not be true.

Generalization

Generalization is a bottom-up process. Generalization is the process of defining a more general entity set from a set of many subtype entity sets. Generalization is a bottom-up process. Subtype entity sets are combined to show that a general entity is obtained by combining two or more subtype entity sets. Generalization and specialization are opposite to each other.

Specialization

Specialization is the process of defining one or more subtype entity sets from a supertype entity set. Specialization is a top-down process. It is the reverse process of the generalization.

Constraints in supertype/subtype relationships :

Possible constraints are given below:

1. Completeness Constraints
   a. Total specialization constraint
   b. Partial specialization constraint
2. Disjointness Constraints
   a. Disjoint constraint
   b. Overlapping constraint

Total specialization rule

Every employee in the supertype must be either full time or par time employee. Double lines indicate total specialization rule. Employee_type is called subtype discriminator. Subtypes can have additional attributes also.

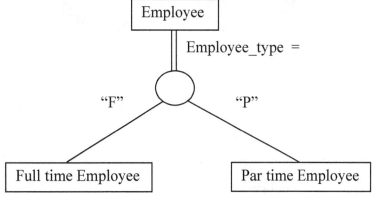

Figure 6.2 Total specialization rule

Partial specialization rule

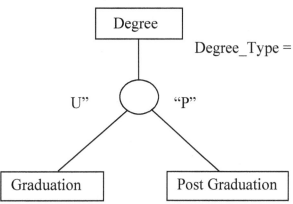

Figure 6.3 Partial specialization rule

Every degree in the supertype may or may not belong to any one of the subtypes. Single line indicates partial specialization rule. For example, Ph.D is a degree but it is neither UG nor PG. Hence, Ph.D entities exists in supertype but not exists in subtypes. Disjoint constraint

Every supertype entity degree must belong to either UG or PG but not both. d stands for disjoint.

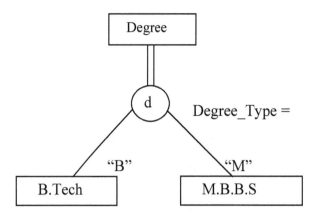

Figure 6.4 Disjoint constraint

Overlapping rule

There are some employees who work as full time employees during regular hours and par time employees in extra ours. Such employees may come in both subtypes. It is called overlapping rule. Every employee must belong to at least one subtype. It satisfies total participation and overlapping constraints. o stands for overlap.

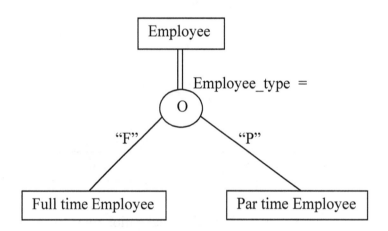

Figure 6.5 Overlapping rule

6.5 Aggregation

Aggregation is a high level abstract concept that is used for building composite or complex objects from their component objects.

6.5.1 First type of aggregation

Aggregate all attribute values of an object in order obtain the whole object. Aggregation is also used to construct a relationship between relationships. Student record is an aggregation of the component attributes – Admission_no, Student_name,

Join_date

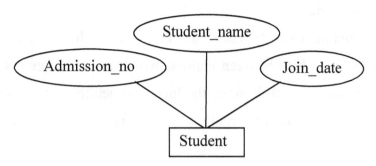

Figure 6.6 Aggregation

6.5.2 Second type of aggregation is abstracting a relationship between objects (entity sets) and viewing the relationship as an object (relationship set)

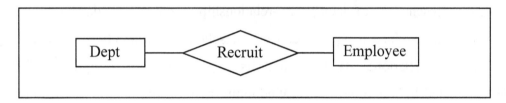

Figure 6.7 Aggregated higher level object

Main disadvantage of the ER data model is that it is not possible to represent relationship among relationships. Aggregation is an abstraction and by using aggregation relationships are treated as higher level entities. Aggregation groups a part of an ER diagram into a single entity set.

Aggregation creates relationship between relationship sets. That is, aggregation is used to express a relationship among relationships.

6.6 Entity-Relationship (ER) data model and Entity-Relationship Diagrams (ERDs)

The Entity Relationship (ER) Data Model

Entity-Relationship (ER) data model, a high-level data model that is useful in developing a conceptual design for a database. Creation of an ER diagram, which is one of the first steps in designing a database, helps the designer(s) to understand and to specify the desired components of the database and the relationships among those components. An ER data model is pictorially represented by an ER diagram (ERD) containing entities, relationships among them, and attributes of the entities and the relationships. The ER data model is one of several semantic data models. It represents meaning of data. ER data model is popular data model for high level database design and it is widely used to develop initial database design. ER data model is used in conceptual database design.

ERD is a data modeling technique that creates a graphical representation of the entities, and the relationships between entities, within an information system. Entity Relationship Diagrams (ERDs) illustrate the logical structure of databases. An entity-relationship (ER) diagram is a specialized graphic that illustrates the relationships between entities in a database.

Entity Relationship Diagrams (ERD) should be the starting point of all software development projects.

In software engineering, an entity-relationship model (ERM) is an abstract and conceptual representation of data. Entity-relationship modeling is a database modeling method, used to produce a type of conceptual schema or semantic data model of a system, often a relational database, and its requirements in a top-down fashion. Diagrams created by this process are called entity-relationship diagrams, ER diagrams, or ERDs.

An ER diagram is a diagram that helps to design databases in an efficient way. Conceptual Modeling is an important phase in designing a successful database. A conceptual data model is a set of concepts that describe the structure of a database and associated retrieval and updating transactions on the database. A high level model is chosen so that all the technical aspects are also covered.

The ER data model grew out of the exercise of using commercially available DBMSs to model the database. The ER model is the generalization of the earlier available commercial models like the Hierarchical and the Network Model. It also allows the representation of the various constraints as well as their relationships. ERD represent the elements of the conceptual model that show the meanings and the relationships between those elements independent of any particular DBMS and implementation details.

ER model is based on a view of a real world that consists of set of objects called entities and relationships among entity sets which are basically a group of similar objects. The relationships between entity sets is represented by a named ER relationship and is of 1:1, 1: N or M: N type which tells the mapping from one entity set to another. Features of the ER Model:

1. The ER diagram used for representing ER Model can be easily converted into Relations (tables) in Relational Model.

2. The ER Model is used for the purpose of good database design by the database developer to use that data model in various DBMS.

3. It is helpful as a problem decomposition tool as it shows the entities and the relationship between those entities.

4. It is inherently an iterative process. On later modifications, the entities can be inserted into this model.

5. It is very simple and easy to understand by various types of users and designers because specific standards are used for their representation.

Ovals are used to represent attributes. Diamonds are normally used to represent relationships.

Entity

An entity is an object or concept about which you want to store information. An entity may be a physical object such as a house or a car, an event such as a house sale or a car service, or a concept such as a customer transaction or order. An entity, strictly speaking, is an instance of a given entity-set. There are usually many instances of an entity-set

An entity is an identifiable real-world item or concept that exists on its own. The entity is a person, object, place or event for which data is collected.

An attribute of an entity is a particular property that describes the entity. The set of all possible values of an attribute is the attribute domain.

Sometimes the value of an attribute is unknown or missing, and sometimes a value is not applicable. In such cases, the attribute can have the special value of null. Null is the special attribute value that indicates an unknown or missing value.

An attribute or set of attributes that uniquely identifies a particular entity is a key.

An entity is a person or place or object or thing in the real world that is uniquely identifiable from all other real world objects. An entity has a set of properties. Entities are two types concrete such as place, person, object etc and abstract such as account, course, results etc. In short we can say that any identifiable object (person, place, thing, concept) in the real world is called an entity. An entity is described by a set of attributes. Entity set

A collection of similar entities is called an entity set. All entities in a given entity set will have same attribute names and same number of attributes. Collection of similar entities with same attributes is called an entity set. For example set of students in the class, set accounts in the bank, set of employees in an organization are examples of entity sets. An entity set is also known as entity type. An entity in the entity set is called entity instance.

Attribute

An attribute is a property or characteristic of an entity. An entity is described or represented by a set of attributes.

Domain of an attribute

The set of permissible values of an attribute is called its domain. Two or more attributes in the same relation can have same domains

Types of attributes

Component or simple or atomic attribute

An attribute that cannot be further subdivided into subparts is called a simple attribute.

Composite attribute

An attribute that can be further subdivided into sub parts is called composite attribute. For example, address is a composite attribute. Houseno, StreetName, Townname and StateName are called component or simple attributes.

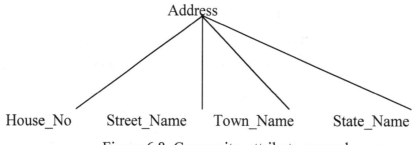

Figure 6.8 Composite attribute example

Derived attribute

Derived attribute is also known as calculated attribute. A derived attribute can be obtained from other attributes. When the value of an attribute is derived from the values of other related attributes or entities then that attribute is called derived attribute. . For example, an employee's monthly salary is based on the employee's annual salary.

Identifier attribute

An identifier is an attribute or set of attributes used to uniquely identify an entity in the entity set. An identifier containing single attribute is called simple identifier. An identifier containing more than one attribute is called composite identifier.

Single-valued attribute

If a particular attribute of a particular entity contains only one value then it is called single valued attribute.

Multi valued attributes

A multivalued attribute can have more than one value for a given entity. For example, an employee entity can have multiple skill values. Here skill is a multivalued attribute.

Htno	Student_name	Account	Economic	Computers	Total	Skill
789	C. Hemanth	100	100	100	300	chess, dance, cricket
699	D. Arya	99	99	99	297	Cricket
321	P. Thejesh	88	88	88	264	NULL
345	C. Ramya	60	60	60	180	artist, driving

Table 6.1

- Htno, Student_name, accounts, economics, computers - are single valued attributes.
- Skill is multivalued attribute and
- Total, average are derived or calculated attribute

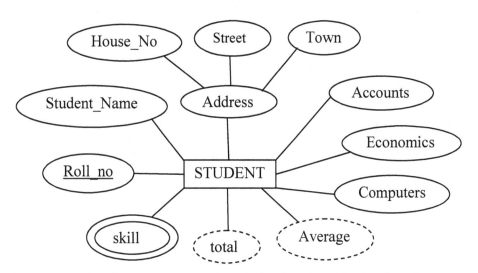

Figure 6.9 STUDENT ER diagram- composite, derived and multivalued attributes

Address is composite attribute. Skill is multivalued attribute. Total and average are derived attributes. All other attributes are simple attributes.

Relationship

A relationship is a mapping or an association between or among entities of the same entity set or different entity sets. A relationship captures how two or more entities are related to one another

Relationship set

A relationship set is a set of associations among entity sets. A set of similar relationships or collection of similar relationships is called a relationship set. An instance of a relationship set is a set of or collection of relationships. Attributes that are connected to relationship sets are called descriptive attributes.

Degree of the relationship set

The number of entity sets that participate in a relationship set is known as the degree of the relationship set.

In ER diagram the mapping between entities is called mapping cardinalities or cardinality ratios. There are four types of possible mapping cardinalities

1. One-to-one
2. One-to-many
3. Many-to-one
4. Many-to-many

Mapping cardinality specifies the number of entities in one entity set that are directly associated with number of entities in another entity set through a relationship set.

One-to-one mapping cardinality

Each manager manages only one department. For every department there should be only one manager. The relationship between a department and a manager is one-to-one. That is, there is only one manager per department and a manager manages only one department.

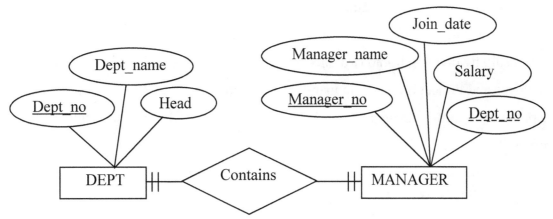

Figure 6.10 one-to-one relationship

Sales ——————————————Rama Krishna

Accounting ————————————Suresh

Purchase ————————————Pratap

Finance   Thegesh

One-to-one instance of a relation

One-to-many mapping cardinality

Mapping cardinality is one to many from DEPT to EMPLOYEE and many to one from EMPLOYEE to DEPT.

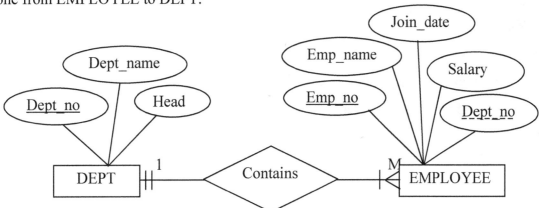

Figure 6.11 One-to-many relationship

A department can have many employees but each employee belongs to one and only one department.

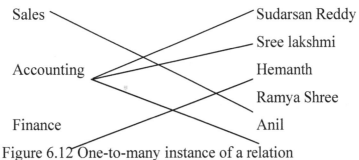

Figure 6.12 One-to-many instance of a relation

Many-to-many mapping cardinality

Many-to-many relationships should be avoided. We can resolve a many-to-many relationship by dividing it into two one-to-many relationships. The relationship between Employee and Project is a many to many relationship.

Mapping cardinality is many to many from STUDENT to SUBJECT and many to many from SUBJECT to STUDENT.

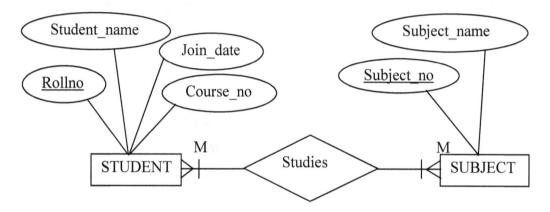

Figure 6.13 many-to-many relationship

A student is allowed to study many subjects and many students are allowed to study the same subject.

KEYS

Super key

A super key is a set of one or more attributes and that set is used to uniquely identify an entity in the entity set.

Candidate key (minimal super key)

An entity set can have any number of super keys. Minimal super keys are called candidate keys. Minimal super key is a super key for which there is no subset. An entity set can have any number of candidate keys.

Primary key

Every entity set should contain one and only one primary key. Every primary key is also a candidate key but every candidate key is need not be a primary key. A primary key is a set of one or more attributes and that set is used to uniquely identify an entity in the entity set. For a particular entity set a candidate key that is selected by the database designer is called a primary key.

Strong entity set

An entity set containing a primary key is called strong entity set. Strong entity set exists independently of other entity sets. A strong entity set can exist by its own. In real life, by nature, most of the real life entity sets are strong entity sets only.

Weak entity set

An entity set that contains no primary key is called weak entity set. A weak entity set is always existence depends on some other strong entity set. A weak entity set cannot exist by its own. Weak entity sets are used very rarely. Weak entity set contains discriminator or a partial identifier.

Identifying relationship

The relationship between strong entity set and a weak entity set is called an identifying relationship (IR). Strong entity set in an identifying relationship is called identifying owner. For example, in the following entity relationship (ER) diagram Student entity set is a strong entity set and Fee entity set is a weak entity set. Roll_no is a primary key for Student. Payment_no is a partial identifier for Fee. We use double underline to indicate partial identifier. A weak entity set is always existence dependent on some other strong entity set.

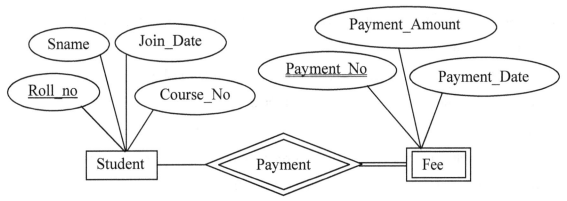

Figure 6.14 Identifying Relationship – Relationship between strong and weak entity sets

Unary relationship example

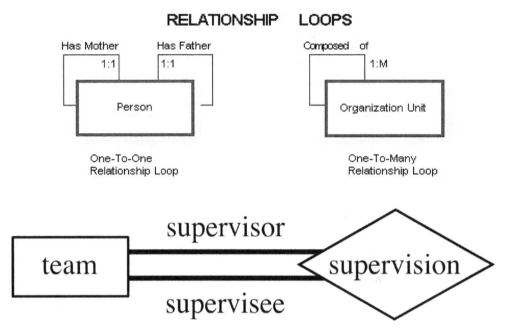

One-to-One and One-to-Many recursive relationship

A unary relationship is a relationship between entities of the same entity set. Unary relationships are also known as recursive relationships. Recursive relationships are rare in nature. We use recursive relationships occasionally. When recursive relationships are defined, we must specify roll indicators clearly so that there will not be any ambiguities in relationships.

Employee reports to Employee. This type of relationship is called a recursive relationship. One person has one mother is a recursive relationship. One person has one father is a recursive relationship. One person has one head is a recursive relationship. One organization unit consists of many organizational units. One student may have many own text books. One student may have many fingers.

Binary relationship

Binary relationship is a relationship between entities of two different entity sets. Binary relationship is the most popular and useful relationship in data modeling. In real life, we find that more than 90% of the relationships are binary relationships only.

Ternary relationship

A ternary relationship is a simultaneous relationship among the entities of three different entity sets. Ternary relationships are used rarely.

6.7 Modeling Conceptual Objects versus Physical Objects

Complexity increases from conceptual modeling to physical modeling.

Modeling Conceptual Objects

Conceptual objects are modeled by using high level components such as entities, entity sets, relationships among the entities, rules, constraints etc. Different diagrams are used to model the conceptual objects. These diagrams include entity relationship (ER) model diagrams, process flow diagrams (PFD), server model diagrams, unified modeling language (UML) class diagrams etc.

Modeling Physical Objects

Physical objects are modeled by physical data models (PDMs). A physical object modeling specifies how to implement conceptual data objects in the database of choice. Conceptual data model is transformed into physical data model that contains relational database with tables, columns, and constraints etc. Physical object modeling involves the actual design of a database according to the requirements specified in conceptual modeling. Physical modeling deals with the conversion of conceptual into a relational data model.

When physical modeling occurs, objects are being defined at the schema level. A schema is a group of related objects in a database. PDM is used to define the database design, PDM shows actual physical details of the database system. A PDM should also indicate the data types for the columns of the relations. Constraints such as primary key, foreign key etc are also defined.

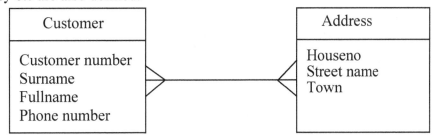

Figure 6.1 A sample conceptual object data model

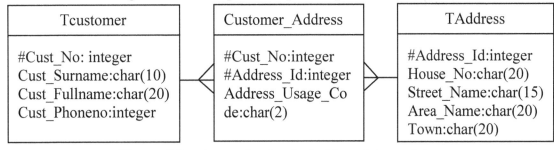

Figure 6.2   A sample physical object data model

99

6.8 Entity Relationship Diagram (ERD) Example of University College

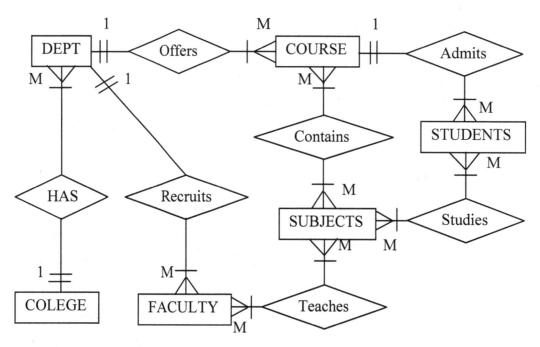

Figure 6.1 Entity Relationship Diagram (ERD) for university college

ENTITY SETS DETAILS ARE

COLLEGE(college_no, college_name, principal_name)

DEPT(dept_no, dept_name, dept_head, college_no)

COURSE(course_no, course_name, fee, duration, dept_no)

STUDENTS(htno, student_name, join_date, course_no)

SUBJECTS(subject_no, subject_name)

FACULTY(faculty_no, faculty_name, join_date, salary, dept_no)

RELATIONSHIP SETS DETAILS ARE

       Contains(course_no, subject_no)

       Studies(student_no, subject_no)

       Teaches(faculty_no, subject_no)

Two relations are created for one-to-many relationships.

Three relations are created for many-to-many relationships.

6.9 Self Assessment Questions

6.9.1 Short Answer Questions

1. List different types of conceptual database models.

2. What is aggregation? Give one example.

3. What is an entity?

4. What is an entity set?

5. What is a relationship set?

6. What is EER database modeling? Give one example.

7. Differentiate between strong entity set and weak entity set.

6.9.2 Essay Questions

1. Explain in detail principles of conceptual database design

2. Explain entity relationship (ER) data model and entity relationship diagrams (ERDs) with examples.

3. What are the advantages of conceptual database models?

4. Explain modeling conceptual objects versus physical objects with examples.

5. Explain identifying relationship with an example.

6. Draw an entity relationship diagram (ERD) for university

7. Draw an entity relationship diagram (ERD) for hospital

8. Draw an entity relationship diagram (ERD) for bus reservation

9. Draw an entity relationship diagram (ERD) for flight reservation

CHAPTER 7

RELATIONAL DATA MODEL AND NORMALIZATION

Objectives

- ✓ To understand relational data model (RDM)
- ✓ To know about the benefits of relational data model (RDM)
- ✓ To know about relational keys
- ✓ To study integrity constraints
- ✓ To know how to convert ER diagrams into relations
- ✓ To understand functional dependencies
- ✓ To study normalization

Chapter Structure

7.1   Introduction

7.2   Relational Data Model (RDM)

7.3   Relational Keys

7.4   Integrity Constraints

7.5   Converting Entity Relationship Diagrams (ERDs) Into Relations

7.6   Functional Dependencies (FDs)

7.7   Normalization

7.8   Self assessment questions

7.1 Introduction

Most database management systems (DBMSs) are based on relational data model (RDM). The relational data model is based on a mathematical concept known as a relation.

7.2 Relational Data Model (RDM)

A Relational database stores data in **tables**. The data stored in a table is organized into rows and columns. Each row in a table represents an individual record and each column represents a field. A **record** is an individual entry in the table. For example, each person's name, address, and phone number is a single record of information in a phone book. Whereas a "**field**" is a basic unit of information in a record. For example, you can divide a person's record in the phone book into fields for their last name, first name, address, city and phone number.

7.2.1 Benefits of a Relational Database

Following are some of the advantages of a relational database:

1. Data independence
2. Data can be easily accessed.
3. Data can be shared.
4. Data modeling can be flexible.
5. Data storage and redundancy can be reduced.
6. Data inconsistency can be avoided.
7. Data Integrity can be maintained.
8. Standards can be enforced.
9. Security restrictions can be applied.
10. Independence between physical storage and logical data design can be maintained.
11. High-level data manipulation language (SQL) can be used to access and manipulate data.

7.2.2 Properties of relations

1. Each relation in a database has a unique name.
2. No two rows are identical in the relation.
3. Each attribute of a relation has unique name.
4. The order or sequence of rows in a relation is not significant.
5. The order or sequence of attributes in a relation is not important.
6. The value at the intersection of each row and each column must be atomic (or single or simple or scalar or indivisible)
7. Multi valued attributes and composite attributes are not allowed in a relation.

Note all relations are tables but all tables need not be relations.

A relational database consists of a collection of tables or relations and each relation should have a unique name and each relation contains a set of attributes with each attribute having unique name. Each attribute of a relation has a distinct name. The relation is the only data structure used in the relational data model.

Relational database management systems (RDBMSs) are the most widely used database management systems now-a-days. A relation is a set of records or rows. Rows of a relation are also called records or tuples or entities. Columns of a relation are also called fields or attributes or items. Each record describes one student in the relation STUDENT. Integrity constraints are conditions or rules that the rows or records in a relation must satisfy. Integrity constraints increase the accuracy of data values in the fields of a relation.

Examples of relational database management systems (RDBMSs) are – DB2, ORACLE, M.S. SQL SERVER, INFORMIX, SYBASE, M.S. ACCESS, FOXBASE, PARADOX, TERADATA, INGRESS, MYSQL etc.

A data definition language (DDL) is used to define the external and logical schemas. SQL is the most widely used database language. SQL is a fourth generation language.

The relational data model represents data in the form of relations. Components of relational data model are:

1. Data structure (the relation containing rows and columns,
2. Data manipulation (using DML commands),
3. Data integrity (applying rules on the data stored in the database).

In relational data model a database is a collection of one or more relations. A relation is a main data structure or construct for storing data. A relation contains rows (records) and columns (attributes).

An instance of a relation is a set of records or tuples or rows or entities.

The degree of a relation is the number of attributes of the relation. Degree of the relation is also called arity of the relation. The cardinality of a relation instance is the number of records in the relation.

A relation schema specifies the domain of each attribute in the relation instance.

DDL stands for data definition language. DDL is a part of the structured query language (SQL). DDL is used to create, modify, delete and drop relations, views, indexes, primary keys, foreign keys, stored procedures, triggers etc. in the database.

The foreign key in the referencing relation must match the primary key of the referenced relation. Foreign key must have the same number of columns and compatible data types with the corresponding primary key but the column names may be same or different.

The entity relationship (ER) data model is the most powerful, most important and convenient tool for representing an initial, high-level database design. An entity set and only selected relationship sets are converted into relations. View data is not actually stored in the database and view data is obtained on the fly from the definition of the view. Views are mainly used for data security purpose.

7.3 Relational Keys

7.3.1 key

A key is an attribute (also known as column or field) or a combination of attributes that is used to identify a record uniquely.

7.3.2 Super Key

An attribute or a collection of one or more attributes that is used to identify a record uniquely in the relation is known as Super Key. A relation can have many Super Keys.

7.3.3 Candidate key

A **candidate key** is any field, or combination of fields, that uniquely identifies a record in one relation. The field or fields of the candidate key must contain unique values (if the values in a key were duplicated, they would be no longer identify unique records), and cannot contain a null value. It can be defined as minimal Super Key or irreducible Super Key. In other words an attribute or a collection of one or more attributes that identifies the record uniquely in the relation but none of its proper subsets can identify the records uniquely in the relation.

7.3.4 Primary key

A primary key is an attribute or set of attributes that uniquely identifies each row (or record) in a relation. A **primary key** is the candidate key that has been chosen by the database designer to identify unique records in a particular relation. A Candidate Key that is selected by the database designer for unique identification of each row in a relation is known as Primary Key. Database designer can use one of the Candidate Key as a Primary Key. A Primary Key can consist of one or more attributes of a relation. Every relation should contain one and only one primary key. A relation cannot have more than one primary key.

7.3.5 Simple primary key

A primary key that contains only one attribute is called a simple primary key.

7.3.6 Composite Primary Key

If a Primary Key contains more than one attribute then that Primary Key is called composite Primary Key (also called a Compound Key or Concatenated Key). That is, a primary key that contains more than one attribute is called composite primary key.

7.3.7 Unique Key

A relation can have one and only one primary key. That is, a relation cannot have more than one primary key. In those cases where a relation needs to have more than one primary key, we use UNIQUE key. UNIQUE allows null values, whereas a primary does not allow null values. A relation can have any number of UNIQUE keys.

7.3.8 Foreign key

A **foreign key** is a reference to a key in another relation. A relationship between two relations is created by creating a common field or fields to the two tables. Foreign keys allow us to ensure what is called "referential integrity". This means a foreign key that contains a value must refer to an existing record in the related relation.

A foreign key is an attribute or combination of attributes in one relation that points to the candidate key (generally it is the primary key) of another relation. The purpose of the foreign key is to ensure referential integrity of the data i.e. only values that are supposed to appear in the database are permitted.

A foreign key is used to represent the relationship between two relations in the same database. A foreign key is an attribute or set of attributes in a relation of a database that acts or works as the primary key of another relation in the same database.

7.3.9 Alternate Key

Alternate Key can be any of the Candidate Keys except the Primary Key.

7.3.10 Secondary Key

The keys that are not even the Super Keys but can be still used for identification of records (not unique) are known as Secondary Keys.

In relational database design, a unique key can uniquely identify each row or record in a relation. A unique key can have one or more attributes. No two distinct rows or records in a relation can have the same value in those attributes if NULL values are not used. Depending on its design, a relation may have many unique keys but at most one primary key.

Unique keys do not enforce the NOT NULL constraint in practice. Because NULL is not an actual value (it represents the lack of a value), when two rows are compared, and both rows have NULL in a column, the column values are not considered to be equal. Thus, in order for a unique key to uniquely identify each row in a table, NULL values must not be used.

A relation can have at most one primary key, but more than one unique key. A primary key is a combination of columns which uniquely identify a row. It is a special case of unique keys. One difference is that primary keys have an implicit NOT NULL constraint while unique keys do not. Thus, the values in unique key columns may or may not be NULL, and in fact such a column may contain at most one NULL fields. Unique keys as well as primary keys can be referenced by foreign keys.

7.4 Integrity Constraints

The simplest type of integrity constraint is specifying a data type for each attribute in the relation. In relational data model data accuracy and data integrity are controlled by using integrity constraints. Different types of integrity constraints are:

1. Domain integrity constraints
2. Entity integrity constraints
3. Referential integrity constraints
4. Action assertions

Domain integrity constraints

Set of allowable values for an attribute of a relation is called its domain. Sometimes allowable range of values of an attribute is specified. Data type and data size are components of a domain. Examples for domain integrity constraints are – null, not null, and check constraints.

Domain integrity ensures that only valid values are assigned to each data item.

Entity integrity constraints

Entity integrity constraint rule says that null values are not allowed in a primary key. That is, a primary key attribute or component of a primary key attribute cannot have null value. Null means nothing. Null is not equal to zero. Null means attribute value is not known. When there is no applicable value for an attribute then it is called null value. In general null values are not allowed.

Referential integrity constraints

A foreign key in one relation directly references a primary key of the same relation or another relation. There are two possible values for a foreign key. Either the foreign key value is null or the foreign key value should match the primary key value of the referenced relation. A referential integrity constraint is a rule that maintains consistency between two relations in the same database.

Action assertions

Assertions are complex integrity constraints or rules on the data of the database. Well-Structured relations

Well structured relation does not mean that the relation contains hundred percent free of redundancies. It may have minimal redundancy and it is easy to insert, modify and delete data in the relation without creating problems called anomalies such as errors or inconsistencies in the data.

- A problem in inserting data into the relation is called insertion anomaly.

- A problem in modification of data in the relation is called modification anomaly.

- A problem in deletion of data in the relation is called deletion anomaly.

7.5 Converting Entity Relationship Diagrams (ERDs) Into Relations

7.5.1 Strong entity set

Name of the entity set is same as the relation name. Attribute names in the entity set are same as the column names in the relation. Identifier or primary key of the entity set is same as the primary key of the relation. STUDENT strong entity set is contains four attributes with student_id as the primary key attribute or identifier. For example, STUDENT strong entity set is converted into relation as follows:

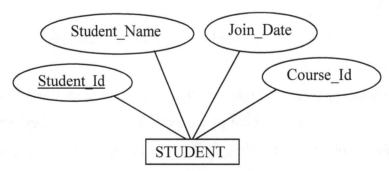

Figure 7.1 STUDENT entity set

Student_Id	Student_Name	Join_Date	Course_Id
9988	Dharma	12-Jan-1989	B.Tech
8877	Bheema	23-Dec-1999	M.Tech
7766	Arjuna	16-Jun-2001	MCA
6655	Nakula	30-Aug-2004	MBA
5544	Sahadeva	22-Mar-2006	B.Com

Table 7.1 STUDENT relation

7.5.2 Strong entity set with composite attribute

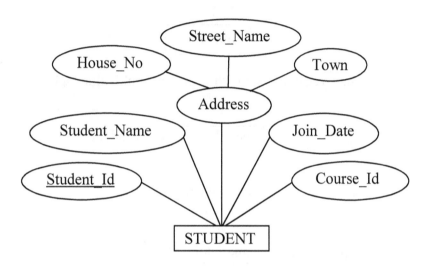

Figure 7.2   STUDENT entity set with composite attribute

When a strong entity set contains a composite attribute you have to create a separate column for each simple attribute and a separate column for each component of the composite attribute. For example, STUDENT entity set with address as composite attribute is converted into a relation as follows:

Student_Id	Student_Nam	Join_Date	Course_I	House_N	Street	Town
9988	Dharma	12-Jan-1989	B.Tech	3-45-2	T.K.stree	Tirupati
8877	Bheema	23-Dec-	M.Tech	23-33-4	Gandhi	Delhi
7766	Arjuna	16-Jun-2001	MCA	1-2-33	Nehru	Piler
6655	Nakula	30-Aug-	MBA	5-6-69	Ramstree	Nellore
5544	Sahadeva	22-Mar-	B.Com	4-66-77	rstreet	Tirumal

Table 7.2 STUDENT relation

7.5.3 Entity set with multivalued attributes.

When a strong entity set contains multivalued attributes two relations are created and these relations are related with primary key, foreign key relationship. For example, employee can have many degrees. Attribute degrees is a multivalued attribute. In entity relationship diagram (ER), multivalued attribute is represented by using double ellipses as shown below:

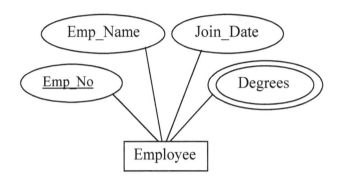

Figure 7.3 Employee entity set with degree as multivalued attribute

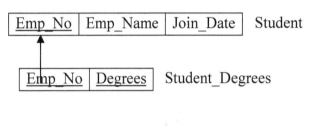

Emp_No	Emp_Name	Join_Date
9999	Sudarsan	16-Jan-2002
8888	Hemanth	26-Dec-2010

Employee

Emp_No	Degrees
9999	B.Tech
9999	M.Tech
9999	Ph.D
8888	MBA
8888	Ph.D
7777	B.Com

Emp_Degree

7.5.4 Weak entity set

Weak entity set is converted into a relation that includes all attributes of the weak entity set and the primary key of the strong entity set on which the weak entity set depends

Primary key of this new relation corresponding to the weak entity set is the union of the primary key of the strong entity set and discriminator (or partial identifier) of the weak entity set.

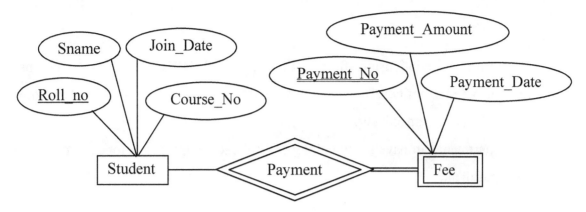

Figure 7.4 Identifying relationship

Roll_no	Sname	Join_date	Course_no
4567	Ravi	3-jan-2001	10
6679	java	6-jun-2005	20
2345	kumari	5-may-2002	10
6666	chitti	9-nov-1999	30

Roll_no	Payment_No	Payment_Amount	Payment_Date
4567	1	2000	24-jan-2001
4567	2	4500	24-jun-2002
4567	3	3500	24-jun-2003
6679	1	6400	10-july-2005
6679	2	3600	10-july-2006
2345	1	1000	16-may-2002
2345	2	2000	16-may-2003
2345	3	3000	16-may-2004
2345	4	4000	16-may-2005
6666	1	10000	24-nov-1999

Roll_no	Sname	Join_date	Course_no

Roll_no	Payment_No	Payment_Amount	Payment_Date

7.5.5 Binary relationships

Binary one-to-many relationships

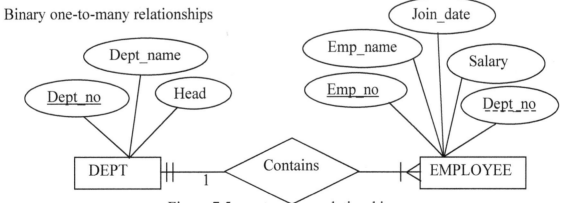

Figure 7.5 one-to-many relationship

111

One-to-many relationship from DEPT to EMPLOYEE – Create relations separately for both the entity sets. Create primary key and foreign key relationship from one side to many side respectively.

A department can have many employees but each employee belongs to one and only one department.

Dept

Dept_no	Dept_name	Head
10	Computer Science	Sudarsan
20	Management	Hemanth
30	Commerce	Suresh

Employee

Emp_no	Emp_name	Join_date	Salary	Dept_n
1111	Dr. Bhagavan	12-Jan-1979	56000	30
2222	Dr. V. Vasudeva Reddy	26-Dec-1989	52000	30
3333	C. Sudarsana Reddy	16-Aug-1999	36000	10
4444	Y. Sree Lakshmi	26-Jan-2006	26000	20
5555	C. hemanth	15-Sep-2009	29000	20

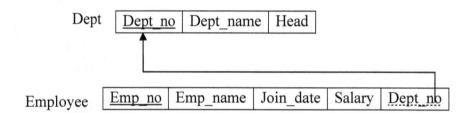

Binary one-to-one relationships

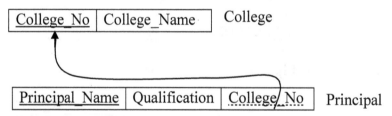

Create one relation for each entity set and then create primary key and foreign key relationship between two relations either from first relation to second relation or second relation to first relation.

Binary many-to-many relationship

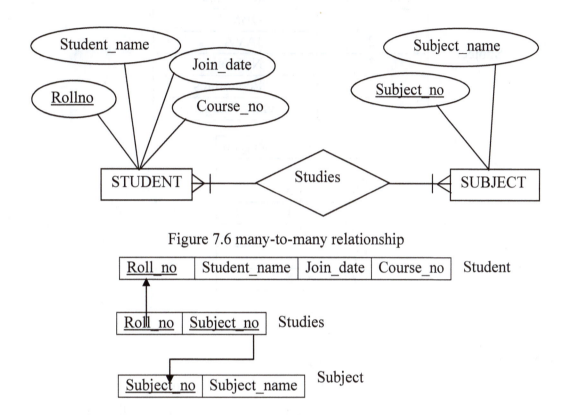

Figure 7.6 many-to-many relationship

| Roll_no | Student_name | Join_date | Course_no | Student |

| Roll_no | Subject_no | Studies |

| Subject_no | Subject_name | Subject |

Create three relations one relation for first entity set; another relation for second entity set and the third relation corresponding to the relationship set.

The primary key of the third relation (relationship set) is the union of the primary key of the two participating entity sets and descriptive attributes of the relationship set.

Sample instances of relations Student, Subject, studies are given below:

Roll_no	Student_name	Join_date	Course_no
9999	Raghu Rama	12-Oct-2005	10
8888	Rajeswari	30-Feb-2006	10
7777	Prsad	24-Mar-2008	20
6666	Anil	6-Apr-2009	30

Student

	Subject_no	Subject_name
Subject	1	DBMS
	2	JAVA
	3	Networks
	4	Economics
	5	Financial Management

	Roll_no	Subject_no
	9999	4
	9999	5
	8888	1
Studies	7777	3
	7777	4
	7777	5
	6666	2
	6666	1

7.5.6 Unary one-to-many relationship

Unary relationships are also called recursive relationships. A unary relationship is defined as a relationship between the entities of the same or single entity set. One manager manages many employees in the employee relation. So, there is a one-to-many relationship from manager to employee.

EMPLOYEE

Emp_No	Emp_Name	Join_Date	Manager_Id	Sal	Deptno
9999	Sudarsan	26-Jun-1996	NULL	7900	10
8888	Hemanth	16-Aug-2002	9999	6600	10
7777	Sri Lakshmi	30-Sep-2001	9999	7600	10
6666	Ramya Shree	5-Mar-2005	9999	5600	10
2999	Suresh	26-May-1997	NULL	7600	20
5555	Bhargav	12-Oct-2003	2999	3500	20

Table 7.3 EMPLOYEE Relation

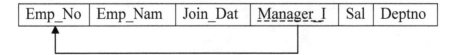

7.6 Functional Dependencies (FDs)

Functional dependency

A functional dependency is a constraint or condition or relationship between two attributes or two sets of attributes in the same relation. Functional dependencies of a relation R are written as follows:

A->A, CE->H, AB->CEH etc.

where A, B, C, E, H are all attributes of the relation R.

A->B reads as A determines B or attribute B is functionally dependent on attribute A. For every valid value of A there exists one and only one value of B. B->A may not be true.

Examples for functional dependencies are:

Htno --> Sname

For any valid hall-ticketno, Htno, there must be one and only one student name

Htno ->{Sname, join-date}

The following functional dependencies

Account_no -> customer_name and

Account_no ->balance

are combined as follows:

Account_no -> {customer_name, balance}

Course_no -> {course_name, fee, duration}

Determinant and dependent

The left hand side and right hand side of a functional dependency are called the determinant and dependent respectively. In Htno -> Sname, Htno is determinant and Sname is dependent.

7.7 Normalization

Database normalization is the process of removing redundant data from relations in order to improve storage efficiency, data integrity, and scalability. In the relational database design the efficiency of a database is quantified by a series of classifications. These classifications are called "normal forms".

In the design process of a relational database management systems (RDBMSs), the process of organizing data to minimize redundancy is called **normalization**. The goal of database normalization is to decompose larger relations with anomalies into smaller, well-structured, less redundant, well organized relations. Normalization usually involves dividing large relations into smaller (and less redundant) relations and defining relationships between them. Through decomposition non-simple domains are replaced by 'domains whose elements are atomic.

Normalization is the process of efficiently organizing data in a database. There are two goals of the normalization process: eliminating redundant data (for example, storing the same data in more than one relation) and ensuring data dependencies make sense (only storing related data in a relation). Both of these are worthy goals as they reduce the amount of storage space a database consumes and ensure that data is logically stored.

The main objective of normalization is to isolate data so that additions, deletions, and modifications of a field can be made in just one relation and then propagated through the rest of the database via the defined relationships.

Normalization Avoids

1. Duplication of Data – The same data is listed in multiple locatiopns of the database

2. Insert Anomaly – A record about an entity cannot be inserted into the table without first inserting information about another entity – Cannot enter a customer without a sales order

3. Delete Anomaly – A record cannot be deleted without deleting a record about a related entity. Cannot delete a sales order without deleting all of the customer's information.

4. Update Anomaly – Cannot update information without changing information in many places. To update customer information, it must be updated for each sales order the customer has placed

Normalization is defined as the process of successively decomposing relations with anomalies into smaller well-structured, well-designed and well-managed relations. The goal of normalization is

- To reduce data redundancy
- To maintain (insert, modify and delete) data very easily
- To improve data design quality
- To represent real world applications with greater accuracy.

7.7.1 First Normal Form (1NF)

A relation is in first normal form (1NF) if a relation contains atomic values only. Atomic means that the intersection of each row and each column should contain single or simple or scalar or indivisible value only. A relation is in INF if multivalued attributes, repeating groups are removed and a primary key has been defined in the relation. Only atomic attribute values are permitted and multivalued attributes and composite attributes are not allowed.

7.7.2 Second Normal Form (2NF)

A relation is in second normal form (2NF) if it is in first normal form (1NF) and contains no partial functional dependencies. If a relation is in 1NF and all partial functional dependencies have been removed in that relation then the relation also in 2NF.

Partial functional dependency means that the relation between part of the primary key and non key attributes in the relation. Partial functional dependency is a functional dependency in which one or more non key attributes of the relation are functionally dependent on part of the primary key of that relation.

If a relation is in first normal form (1NF) but it contains partial functional dependencies then it is not in second normal form (2NF). 1NF relations with partial functional dependencies are converted into 2NF relations as follows:

1. Create new relation for each primary key determinant of the partial functional dependency with determinant as a primary key of the new relation.

2. Move all dependent non-key attributes of that primary key determinant from old relation to new relation.

First normal form relations (1NF) will be in second normal form (2NF) if any one of the following conditions are satisfied.

1. Primary key is a simple primary key. That is primary key contains only one attribute.

2. There are no non key attributes in the relation. Relation contains only primary key attributes.

3. Relation contains only full functional dependencies and no partial functional dependencies.

2NF is based on the concept of full functional dependency.

7.7.3 Third Normal Form (3NF)

A relation is said to be in 3NF if and only if the relation is in 2NF and any transitive dependencies have been removed. A transitive dependency in a relation is a functional dependency between two non key attributes or two sets of non key attributes.

A relation is in third normal form (3NF) if it is in second normal form (2NF) and no transitive dependencies in the relation.

If a relation contains transitive dependencies then the relation is not in third normal form (3NF). Such relations are converted into 3NF relations as follows.

1. Create a new relation for each non key determinant of the transitive dependency. This non key determinant is the primary key of the new relation. Move all dependencies of the transitive dependency form old relation to new relation.

2. Create primary key foreign key relationship from new relation to old relation using determinant as both primary key and foreign key of the new and old relations respectively.

Third normal form (3NF) is based on the concept of transitive dependency.

3NF is widely considered to be sufficient for most applications. Most tables when reaching 3NF are also in BCNF.

7.7.4 Boyce-Codd Normal Form (BCNF)

A relation is in BCNF if it in 3NF and every determinant in the relation is a candidate key. If a relation has only one candidate key, then 3NF and BCNF are equivalent (same). BCNF relation means the relation is in 3NF and any remaining anomalies that result from functional dependencies have been removed.

When a relation is in BCNF, there are no longer any anomalies that result from functional dependencies. Anomalies may exist in a 3NF relation when a relation has more than one candidate key. A relation is in BCNF if and only if every determinant is a candidate key.

1. As the First Normal Form (or 1NF) deals with redundancy of data across a horizontal row, Second Normal Form (or 2NF) deals with redundancy of data in vertical columns.

2. Here we have a one-to-many relationship between the publisher table and the book table. A book has only one publisher, and a publisher will publish many books. When we have a one-to-many relationship, we place a foreign key in the Book Table, pointing to the primary key of the Publisher Table.

3. A table is in 3NF if all of the non-primary key attributes are mutually independent. There should not be transitive dependencies

4. BCNF requires that the table is 3NF and only determinants are the candidate keys.

5. Benefits of normalization – Less storage space , Quicker updates, Less data inconsistency, Clearer data relationships, Easier to add data, Flexible Structure

6. Bad database designs results in redundancy, inefficient storage, anomalies, data inconsistency, difficulties in maintenance.

First Normal Form (1NF) Example

A relation is in first normal form (1NF), if all attribute values are atomic. That is no repeating group, no composite attributes.

In the following relation example (Table 7.4), all attribute values are not atomic –So, the relation is not in first normal form (1NF).

Deptno	Manager_no	Emp_no	Emp_name
10	C.Sudarsana Reddy	2244 3456 4455	Sree Lakshmi Hemanth Ramya Shree
20	D.Suresh Kumar Reddy	9876 8765 7654	CG Bhargav Arya Pratap

Table 7.4

Relation shown in table 7.4 is converted into 1NF relation as follows:

Deptno	Manager_no	Emp_no	Emp_name
10	C.Sudarsana Reddy	2244	Sree Lakshmi
10	C.Sudarsana Reddy	3456	Hemanth
10	C.Sudarsana Reddy	4455	Ramya Shree
20	D.Suresh Kumar Reddy	9876	CG Bhargav
20	D.Suresh Kumar Reddy	8765	Arya
20	D.Suresh Kumar Reddy	7654	Pratap

Table 7.5

Table7.5 is in 1NF. That is all attribute values are atomic because there are no repeating group and no composite attributes.

Second Normal Form (2NF) Example

Consider the relation Emp_Course

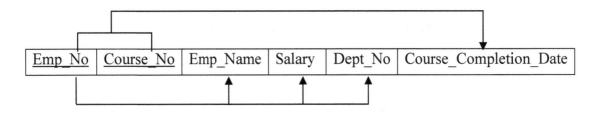

Figure 7.7

Functional dependencies on the relation   Emp_Course are

{Emp_No,Course_No} → Course_Completion_Date   full functional dependency

 Emp_No → { Emp_Name, Salary, Dept_No}   partial functional dependency

Emp_Course   relation is in 1NF but not in 2NF because it contains partial functional dependencies. Hence, Emp_Course relation is normalized as follows:

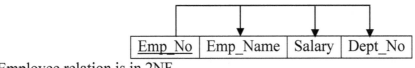

Employee relation is in 2NF

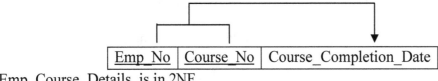

Emp_Course_Details is in 2NF

Figure 7.8

Third Normal Form (3NF) Example

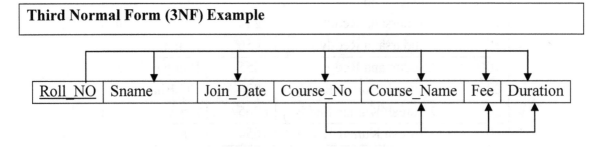

Figure 7.9 Student relation

Student relation is in 2NF, because all values are atomic and there are no partial functional dependencies. But it is not in 3NF, because it contains transitive dependencies. Hence it is normalized as follows:

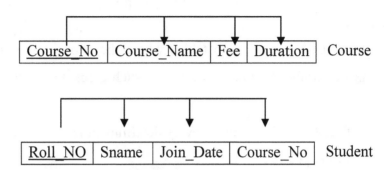

Figure 7.10 Both the relations Course and Student are in 3NF

Boyce-Codd Normal Form (BCNF) Example

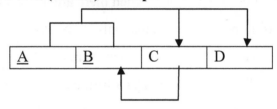

Figure 7.11 A relation that is in 3NF but not in BCNF

Here the primary key is A+B or {A,B}. There is a dependency from a non-key attribute to part of the key. So, the relation is not in BCNF. It can be converted into BCNF as follows:

First change the primary key to A + C or {A,C}

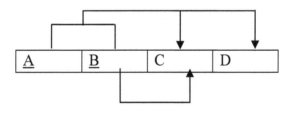

Figure 7.12

This relation is in 1NF but not in 2NF because it contains partial functional dependencies. It is converted into BCNF as follows:

Figure 7.13   3NF and BCNF   3NF and BCNF

NOTE: Consider the relations with the following conditions:

- That had multiple candidate keys.
- Where the multiple candidate keys were composite
- Where the multiple candidate keys overlapped (had at least one attribute to common)

You must understand that in tables where the above three conditions do not apply, you can stop at the third normal form. In such cases, the 3NF is the same as the BCNF.

A relation is in the BCNF if and only if every determinant is a candidate key.

Fourth Normal Form (4NF)

Multivalued dependency

Multivalued dependency exists only when there are at least three attributes in the relation. That means, if a relation contains only two attributes then there are no multivalued attributes in that relation. Assume that there are three attributes A, B, and C in the relation. For each value of A there exists a well defined set of values of B and for each value of A there exists a well defined set of values of C and the set of values of B are independent of the set of values of C.

When a relation contains multivalued dependencies then the relation is not in 4NF. If a relation is in BCNF and any multivalued dependencies have been removed then that relation is in 4NF.

Consider the following relation with the following rules:

1. Each course has a well defined teachers
2. Each course has a well defined text books
3. No relation between teacher and text book. A teacher must be able to teach by using any prescribed text book for that course.

Course	Teacher	Textbook
DBMS	Sudarsan Suresh Pratap	Korth Rama Krishnan
Maths	Hemanth Sree Lakshmi	Prasad Anil

Table 7.6 Relation CTT

122

CTT relation is not in first normal form (1NF). CTT is converted into 1NF as follows:

Relation Course_Teacher_Text is in BCNF

Course	Teacher	Textbook
DBMS	Sudarsan	Korth
DBMS	Sudarsan	Rama krishnan
DBMS	Suresh	Korth
DBMS	Suresh	Rama krishnan
DBMS	Pratap	Korth
DBMS	Pratap	Rama krishnan
Maths	Hemanth	Prasad
Maths	Hemanth	Anil
Maths	Sree Lakshmi	Prasad
Maths	Sree Lakshmi	Anil

Table 7.7 Course_Teacher_Text relation

Relation Course_Teacher_Text is now in 1NF because all values are atomic and primary key is all key. That is, primary key (course, teacher, textbook). When a relation contains only primary key attributes but do not contain non primary key attributes then the relation is in BCNF. Hence, Course_Teacher_Text is in BCNF. Still lot of redundancy is there because of multivalued dependencies. So, it is not in 4NF and there exists anomalies such as

- Insertion is not possible without a prescribed textbook.

- Insertion is not possible without recruiting a teacher.

- If an instructor record is deleted then other details such as course, textbook are also deleted.

- If an instructor is assigned to teach a new course then all corresponding changes must be noted and modified; otherwise modification anomaly exists.

Multivalued dependencies are   Course –>>Teacher, Course –>>Textbook

To remove all the above anomalies above relation is converted into 4NF relation by removing multivalued dependencies as follows:

Course_Teacher Course_Text

Course	Text book
DBMS	Korth
DBMS	Rama krishnan
Maths	Prasad
Maths	Anil

Course	Teacher
DBMS	Sudarsan
DBMS	Suresh
DBMS	Pratap
Maths	Hemanth
Maths	Sree Lakshmi

Table 7.8   Table 7.9

Now, both the relations Course_Teacher and Course_Text are in 4NF. There are no multivalued dependencies in these two relations.

Multivalued dependency is a full constraint between two sets of attributes in a relation. In contrast to the functional dependency, the multivalued dependency requires that certain tuples be present in a relation.

Because the lecturers attached to the course and the books attached to the course are independent of each other, this database design has a multivalued dependency; if we were to add a new book to the DBMS course, we would have to add one record for each of the lecturers on that course, and vice versa.

Put formally, there are two multivalued dependencies in this relation:

{course} $\twoheadrightarrow$ {book} and equivalently {course} $\twoheadrightarrow$ {teacher}.

Databases with multivalued dependencies thus exhibit redundancy.

In database normalization, fourth normal form requires that either every multivalued dependency $X \twoheadrightarrow Y$ is trivial or for every nontrivial multivalued dependency $X \twoheadrightarrow Y$, X is a superkey.

Another Example for 4NF

Emp_Name	Qualifications	Languages
Rama	M.Tech.	C, Java
Bheema	MBA, B.Tech	C, Oracle
Seetha	BA, MA, MBA	Perl,DB2, DataStage

Table 7.10

There is no relationship between qualifications and programming languages

7.8 Self Assessment Questions

7.8.1 Short Answer Questions

1. What is a relation?
2. What are the benefits of the relational data model (RDM)?
3. What is a primary key?
4. What is the difference between primary key and unique key?
5. What is meant by referential integrity?
6. What are functional dependencies? Explain
7. What is normalization?
8. What are the advantages of normalization?
9. Give a relation which is in 3NF but not in BCNF

7.8.2 Essay Questions

1. Explain relational data model (RDM) in detail.
2. What are relational keys? Explain.
3. What are integrity constraints? Explain.
4. Explain the procedure of converting entity relationship diagrams (ERDs) into relations with examples.
5. Explain normalization with examples.
6. Differentiate between 3NF and BCNF
7. Explain fourth normal form (4NF) with an example.

CHAPTER 8

RELATIONAL ALGEBRA AND RELATIONAL CALCULUS

Objectives

- ✓ To study relational algebra
- ✓ To understand relational algebra operations
- ✓ To study relational calculus
- ✓ To understand relational calculus operations

Chapter Structure

8.1   Relational Algebra

8.2   Relational Algebric Operations

8.3   Relational Calculus

8.4   Relational Calculus Operations

8.5   Self assessment questions

8.1 Relational Algebra

Relational algebra is a collection of operations used to manipulate relations (tables). These operations enable the users to specify the retrieval requests which result in a new relation built from one or more relations.

Relational Algebra is a procedural language, which specifies, the operations to be performed on the existing relations to derive result relations. It is a procedural language, which means that user has to specify what is required and what is the sequence of steps performed on the database to obtain the required output. Whenever the operations are performed on the existing relations to produce new relations then the original relations(s) are not affected i.e. they remain the same, and the resultant relation obtained can act as an input to some other operation, so relational algebra operations can be composed together into a relational algebra expression. Composing relational algebra operation into relational expression is similar to composing arithmetic operations (+, -, *) into arithmetic expressions. R1+R2 is a relational expression where R1 and R2 are relations.

It is important that the results of use of relational algebric operations on relations (Tables) must themselves be a relation (Tables). This is because these operators can be used sequentially in various combinations to obtain desired results. Thus each operation on completion must leave data as a relation (table) for the next operator to use. So, this property which all the above operators must have is referred to as relational closure.

Relational Algebra is a formal and non-user friendly language. It illustrates the basic operations required for any data manipulation languages but it is very less commonly used in the commercial languages because it lacks the syntactic details, although it acts as a fundamental technique for extracting data from the database.

8.2 Relational Algebra Operations

The Relational Algebra Operations can be divided into two groups.

1. Basic Set Oriented Operations or Traditional Set Operations – These are derived from Mathematical Set theory. They are applicable because each relation is defined to be set of tuples. These include Union, Intersection, Difference, Cartesian Product. All of these operations are binary operations which means that operation applies to pair of relations.

2. Special relational operations - These include join, selection, projection and division. These operations were designed specifically for relational databases. These operations don't add any power to the relational algebra but simplify for common queries that are lengthy to express using basic set oriented operations.

These operations were introduced by Dr. Codd. But these could not meet all the requirements, so some additional operations were introduced. These included aggregate functions like SUM, AVERAGE, COUNT, OUTER JOIN etc.

Course_no	Course_name	Fee	Duration
10	B.Com	16000	3 years
20	M.C.A	26000	3 years
30	M.Tech	96000	2 years
40	MBA	56000	2 years

Table 8.1 COURSE relation

Roll_no	Student_name	Join_date	Course_no
1111	Sudarsan	20-jan-2002	30
2222	Sri Lakshmi	30-aug-2004	10
3333	Hemanth	16-jun-2001	10
4444	Ramya Shree	2-jan-1999	30
5555	Arya Babu	12-feb-2006	20

Table 8.2 STUDENT relation

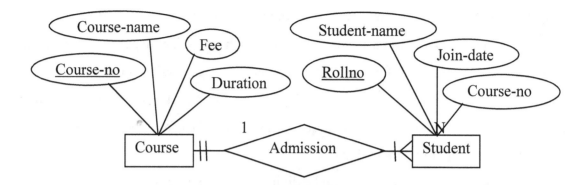

Figure 8.1   ER diagram one-to-many relationship from COURSE to STUDENT

Relational algebra is a formal procedural query language. A query is a question asking data from the database. Query languages are special purpose languages for asking questions or queries. A query consists of collection of operators. The input of a query is a relation instance and the output of a query is also a relation instance.

Basic operators of relational algebra are -selection, projection, Cartesian product, union and difference.

Selection (σ)

The selection operator, σ, selects records from the relation instance. Selection is a unary operator. For example, in the COURSE relation to select all records with course-fee > 15000 the query is

$$\sigma_{course\text{-}fee > 15000}(COURSE)$$

From the COURSE relation to select all records with course-fee > 25000 and course-name is B.Com the query is

$$\sigma_{course\text{-}fee > 25000 \wedge course\text{-}name = \text{'B.Com'}}(COURSE)$$

To display all records except those records whose course-no = 20

$$\sigma_{course\text{-}no \neq 20}(COURSE)$$

PROJECTION (Π)

Projection operator displays only selected columns of a relation. It is a unary operator. Hence, it requires only one argument relation.

The query to display only all values in the course-name column from the relation COURSE

$$\Pi_{course\text{-}name}(COURSE)$$

To display all attribute values of course-no, course-name, course-fee the query is

$$\Pi_{\text{course-no, course-name, fee}}(\text{COURSE})$$

$$\Pi_{\text{course-no, course-name}}(\sigma_{\text{course-fee} > 26500}(\text{COURSE}))$$

Set Operators

UNION (U)

Suppose A and B are two relations. AUB returns a relation instance containing records either from A or B or both. To apply union operation, both argument relations A and B must have the same arity or degree. When the relations A and B have same degree they are called union compatible. It is a binary operator, so it requires two argument relations.

INTERSECTION (∩)

A ∩ B returns a relation instance containing records in both A and B relations. Here also A and B must be union compatible. It is a binary operator, so it requires two argument relations.

CROSS PRODUCT (X)

It is a binary operator. A X B returns all records from both the relations after forming Cartesian product. If a relation A contains m records and the relation B contains n records then the relation A X B contains mn records.

SET DIFFERENCE (–)

It is a binary operator. Let A and B are two relations. A – B returns a relation instance containing records that occur in A but not in B. Both the relations must be union compatible.

RENAME (ρ)

Rename operator is used to rename already existing relation. It is a unary operator.

$$\Pi_{\text{course-name, fee}}(\sigma_{\text{course.fee} < \text{temp.fee}}(\text{COURSE X } \rho_{\text{temp}}(\text{COURSE})))$$

8.3 Relational Calculus

Tuple relational calculus is a non-procedural query language. It describes only the desired information without specifying any procedure how to get the desired information. General form of query in tuple relational calculus is

$$\{ t | P(t) \}$$

129

and it is read as the set of all tuples t such that the predicate P is true for tuple t. P is a formula several tuple variables may appear in a formula.

8.4 Relational Calculus Operations

To display all tuples in the COURSE relation

$$\{ t| t \in COURSE \}$$

To display all tuples in the COURSE relation whose course fee value is > 25000

$$\{ t| t \in COURSE \land t[fee] > 25000 \}$$

To display only all values in the course-name attribute in the COURSE relation

$$\{ t| \exists s \in COURSE (t[course-name]=s[course-name]) \}$$

To display only values in the course-name attribute such that fee value > 25000. That is resultant relation contains only one customer-name column

$$\{ t| \exists s \in COURSE (t[course-name]=s[course-name] \land s[fee]>25000) \}$$

To find names of all students who are studying B.Com course

$$\{ t| \exists s \in STUDENT (t[student-name]=s[student-name]$$
$$\land \exists u \in COURSE (u[course-no]=s[course-no] \land u[course-name]="B.Com")) \}$$

To find student-names in both the relations STUDENT and ENTRANCE

$$\{ t| \exists s \in STUDENT(t[student-name]=s[student-name])$$
$$\land \exists u \in ENTRANCE(t[student-name]=u[student-name]) \}$$

To find student-names either in STUDENT relation or in ENTRANCE relation or in both

$$\{ t| \exists s \in STUDENT(t[student-name]=s[student-name])$$
$$\lor \exists u \in ENTRANCE(t[student-name]=u[student-name]) \}$$

Find all student names in the relation STUDENT but not in the relation ENTRANCE

$$\{ t| \exists s \in STUDENT(t[student-name]=s[student-name])$$
$$\land \neg \exists u \in ENTRANCE(t[student-name]=u[student-name]) \}$$

A tuple variable is said to be a free variable unless it is quantified by a $\exists$ or $\forall$. For example, in the following query or formula

$$t \in STUDENT \land \exists s \in COURSE (t[course-no]=s[course-no])$$

t is a free variable whereas tuple variable s is said to be a bound variable.

Formulas or queries in the tuple relational calculus are constructed by using atoms. Some atoms used in relational calculus are shown below:

- t ∈ TEMP, where t is a tuple variable and TEMP is a relation,
- t[x] = s[x],
- t[x] > s[x],
- t[x] <= s[x],
- t[x] ≠ s[x] etc
- t[x] > 123,
- t[x] <100,
- t[x] ≠1234 etc

Formulas are constructed using atoms and by applying rules as follows:

- An atom is a formula
- If P is a formula then ¬P is also a formula
- If P and Q are two formulas then P V Q, P Λ Q, P V ¬Q, P Λ ¬Q and P => Q are also formulas

Safety formula or safety expressions

There is a possibility of generating infinite relation in tuple relational calculus. Care must be taken to avoid such results.

QUEL (QUERY language) is the data manipulation language for INGRES RDBMS.

8.5 Self Assessment Questions

8.5.1 Short Answer Questions

1. What is relational algebra?
2. What is relational calculus?

8.5.2 Essay Questions

1. Explain relational algebra operators with examples.
2. Explain relational calculus operators with examples.

CHAPTER 9

SQL SCHEMA AND SQL OBJECTS

Objectives

✓ To know about schema, database schema, database instance

✓ To study DDL statements

✓ To understand views

Chapter Structure

9.1 Schema

9.2 Database Schema

9.3 Database Instance

9.4 DDL Statements

9.5 Database Languages

9.6 Views

9.1 Schema

A schema is a description of a particular collection of data, using a given data model.

9.2 Database schema

Overall design of the database is called database schema. A schema is defined as data description in terms of a desired data model or database model. A schema is a template for describing a relation. A schema defines the database and a subschema defines the portion of the database that a specific program will use. Database schema for relational data model is called relational database schema. In the relational data model a schema is defined as

Course-schema (course_no: integer, course_name: string, fee: number, duration:string)

Students-schema(Roll_no:integer,student_name: string, join_date: date, course_no:string)

Schema Overview

A relational database contains a *catalog* that describes the various elements in the system. The catalog divides the database into sub-databases known as schemas. Within each schema there are database objects – tables, views and privileges.

132

The catalog itself is a set of tables with its own schema name - *definition_schema*. Tables in the catalog cannot be modified directly. They are modified indirectly with SQL-Schema statements.

9.3 Database instance

Data stored in the database at a particular time instant is called database instance.

9.4 DDL statements in SQL

The Data Definition Language (DDL) is used to create and destroy databases and database objects.

CREATE

SQL-Schema Statements provide maintenance of catalog objects for a schema – tables, views and privileges. This subset of SQL is also called the Data Definition Language for SQL (SQL DDL).

The CREATE TABLE Statement

The CREATE TABLE statement is used to create a table in a database.

SQL CREATE TABLE Syntax

CREATE   TABLE   table_name

  (

      column_name1   data_type,

      column_name2   data_type,

      column_name3   data_type,

      ....

)

The data type specifies what type of data the column can hold.

Create statement is used to create tables, views, and also used to create functions, stored procedures, triggers, indexes etc.

DROP

Used to totally eliminate a table, view, index from a database - which means that the records as well as the total structure is removed permanently from the database. DROP, allows us to remove entire database objects from our DBMS. For example, if we want to permanently remove the DEPT table the command is

  DROP TABLE DEPT

ALTER

Once you've created a table within a database, you may wish to modify the definition of it. The ALTER command allows you to make changes to the structure of a table without deleting and recreating it. Alter is used to alter or in other words, change the structure of a table, view, index.

```
SQL>  CREATE  TABLE  COURSE
        (
            COURSE_ID        NUMBER(2)      PRIMARY KEY,
            COURSE_NAME   VARCHAR2(10)   NOT NULL,
            FEE                    NUMBER(10,2)   NOT NULL,
            DURATION         VARCHAR2(7)    NOT NULL
        );
Table created.
SQL> CREATE  TABLE  STUDENT
        (
            STUDENT_ID        NUMBER(4)      PRIMARY  KEY,
            STUDENT_NAME  VARCHAR2(15)  NOT NULL,
            JOIN_DATE          DATE               NOT NULL,
            COURSE_ID                               NUMBER(2)   REFERENCES
COURSE(COURSE_ID)
        )
Table created.
SQL> DESCRIBE  COURSE
```

Name	Null?	Type
COURSE_ID	NOT NULL	NUMBER(2)
COURSE_NAME	NOT NULL	VARCHAR2(10)
FEE	NOT NULL	NUMBER(10,2)
DURATION	NOT NULL	VARCHAR2(7)

```
SQL> DESC STUDENT
     Name                          Null?    Type
     ------------------------------ -------- ----------------
     STUDENT_ID                    NOT NULL  NUMBER(4)
     STUDENT_NAME                  NOT NULL  VARCHAR2(15)
     JOIN_DATE                     NOT NULL  DATE
     COURSE_ID                               NUMBER(2)

SQL> create  table  customer
     (
            customer_id    number(6)  primary  key
     );

SQL>  alter table customer add customer_name varchar2(15);

SQL> alter table customer modify customer_name varchar2(15) not null;

SQL> alter table customer add address1 varchar2(10) not null;

SQL> alter table customer add address2 varchar2(10) not null;

SQL> desc customer
     Name                          Null?    Type
     ------------------------------ -------- --------------------------
     CUSTOMER_ID                    NOT NULL NUMBER(6)
     CUSTOMER_NAME                  NOT NULL VARCHAR2(15)
     ADDRESS1                       NOT NULL VARCHAR2(10)
     ADDRESS2                       NOT NULL VARCHAR2(10)

SQL> alter table customer drop column address1;

SQL> desc customer
     Name                          Null?       Type
     ------------------------------ -------- --------------------------
     CUSTOMER_ID                    NOT NULL  NUMBER(6)
     CUSTOMER_NAME                  NOT NULL  VARCHAR2(15)
     ADDRESS2                       NOT NULL  VARCHAR2(10)

SQL>  alter table customer drop column address2;
```

```
SQL> desc customer

        Name                    Null?           Type
        ------------------------------------ -------- ---------------------------
        CUSTOMER_ID             NOT NULL    NUMBER(6)
        CUSTOMER_NAME           NOT NULL    VARCHAR2(15)
SQL> alter table customer add address1 varchar2(10) not null;
SQL> alter table customer add address2 varchar2(10) not null;
SQL> describe customer
        Name                    Null?           Type
        ------------------------------------ -------- ---------------------------
        CUSTOMER_ID             NOT NULL  NUMBER(6)
        CUSTOMER_NAME           NOT NULL  VARCHAR2(15)
        ADDRESS1                NOT NULL  VARCHAR2(10)
        ADDRESS2                NOT NULL  VARCHAR2(10)
SQL>  create table account
      (
            account_no      number(6)       primary key,
            balance         number(10,2)    not null,
            branch_name     varchar2(10)    not null,
            customer_id     number(6) references customer(customer_id)
      )
SQL> describe  account
        Name                    Null?           Type
        ------------------------------------ -------- ---------------------------
        ACCOUNT_NO              NOT NULL    NUMBER(6)
        BALANCE                 NOT NULL    NUMBER(10,2)
        BRANCH_NAME             NOT NULL    VARCHAR2(10)
        CUSTOMER_ID                         NUMBER(6)
SQL>  create table exam    (   htno  number(6)   )
SQL>  desc exam
```

```
        Name                    Null?  Type
        ----------------------------------- ------- --------------------------
        HTNO                              NUMBER(6)
```

SQL> alter table exam add primary key(htno);

SQL> describe exam

```
        Name                    Null?           Type
        ----------------------------------- ------- --------------------------
        HTNO              NOT NULL    NUMBER(6)
```

SQL> alter table exam add exam_name varchar2(10) not null;

SQL> describe exam

```
        Name                    Null?           Type
        ----------------------------------- ------- --------------------------
        HTNO                   NOT NULL     NUMBER(6)
        EXAM_NAME           NOT NULL     VARCHAR2(10)
```

SQL> alter table exam add exam_date date not null;

SQL> describe exam

```
        Name                    Null?           Type
        ----------------------------------- ------- --------------------------
        HTNO                   NOT  NULL        NUMBER(6)
        EXAM_NAME           NOT  NULL        VARCHAR2(10)
        EXAM_DATE           NOT  NULL        DATE
```

SQL> DROP TABLE TEMP;

SQL> create table tenth

        (

            htno number(4) primary key

)

1. create table tablename (column1 datatype, column2 datatype,column3 datatype,...)

2. alter table tablename add column1 data type

3. alter table tablename modify column1 data type

4. drop table tablename

SQL> select * from tab;

no rows selected

9.5 Database Languages

A DBMS is a software package that carries out many different tasks including the provision of facilities to enable the user to access and modify information in the database. The database is an intermediate link between the physical database, computer and the operating system and the users. To provide the various facilities to different types of users, a DBMS normally provides one or more specialized programming languages called database languages.

Database languages come in different forms. They are:

1. Data Definition Language (DDL)
2. Data Manipulation Language (DML)
3. Data Control language (DCL)
4. Transaction Control Language

Data Definition Language (DDL)

As the name suggests, this language is used to define the various types of database objects in the database and their relationship with each other.

The basic functions performed by DDL are:

- Create tables, files, databases and data dictionaries.
- Specify the storage structure of each table on disk.
- Integrity constraints on various tables.
- Security and authorization information of each table.
- Specify the structure of each table.
- Overall design of the Database.

Data Manipulation Language (DML)

A language that enables users to manipulate or access data (insert, update, delete and retrieve) as organized by a certain data model is called the data manipulation language (DML). It can be of two types

1. Procedural DML - It describes what data is needed and how to get it. For example - Relational Algebra.
2. Non Procedural DML - It describes what data is needed without specifying how to get it. For example - SQL or Relational calculus

Definition of SQL

SQL stands for Structured Query Language. It allows access, insert/update/delete records and retrieves data from the database

9.6 Views

Views are known as logical tables. They represent the data of one or more tables. A view derives its data from the tables on which it is based. These tables are called base tables. Views can be based on actual tables or another view also. Whatever DML operations you performed on a view they actually affect the base table of the view. You can treat views same as any other table. You can query, insert, update and delete from views, just as any other table. Views are very powerful and handy since they can be treated just like any other table but do not occupy the space of a table.

The following sections explain how to create, replace, and drop views using SQL commands.

Creating Views

SQL CREATE VIEW Syntax

CREATE VIEW view_name AS SELECT column_name(s) FROM table_name WHERE condition

Suppose we have EMP and DEPT tables. To see the empno, ename, sal, deptno, department name and location we have to give a join query like this.

select e.empno,e.ename,e.sal,e.deptno,d.dname,d.loc

From emp e, dept d where e.deptno = d.deptno;

So every time we want to see employee details and department names where they are working we have to give a long join query. Instead of giving this join query again and again, we can create a view on these tables by using a CREATE VIEW command given below.

create view emp_dept as select e.empno, e.ename,e.sal,e.deptno,d.dname,d.loc

from emp e, dept d where e.deptno = d.deptno;

Now to see the employee details and department names we don't have to give a join query, we can just type the following simple query.

select * from emp_dept;

This will show same result as you have typed the long join query. Now you can treat this EMP_DEPT view same as any other table.

CREATE VIEW accounts_staff AS SELECT Empno, Ename, Deptno FROM Emp WHERE Deptno = 10 WITH CHECK OPTION CONSTRAINT ica_Accounts_cnst;

Now to see the account people you don't have to give a query with where condition you can just type the following query.

Select * from accounts_staff;

Select sum(sal) from accounst_staff;

Select max(sal) from accounts_staff;

CREATE VIEW sup_orders

AS SELECT suppliers.supplier_id, orders.quantity, orders.price FROM suppliers, orders

WHERE suppliers.supplier_id = orders.supplier_id and suppliers.supplier_name = 'IBM';

As you can see how views make things easier.

The query that defines the ACCOUNTS_STAFF view references only rows in department 10. Furthermore, WITH CHECK OPTION creates the view with the constraint that INSERT and UPDATE statements issued against the view are not allowed to create or result in rows that the view cannot select.

Considering the example above, the following INSERT statement successfully inserts a row into the EMP table through the ACCOUNTS_STAFF view:

INSERT INTO Accounts_staff VALUES (110, 'sudarsan', 10);

However, the following INSERT statement is rolled back and returns an error because it attempts to insert a row for department number 30, which could not be selected using the ACCOUNTS_STAFF view:

INSERT INTO Accounts_staff VALUES (111, 'SAMI', 30);

Replacing/Altering Views

To alter the definition of a view, you must replace the view using one of the following methods:

- A view can be dropped and then re-created. When a view is dropped, all grants of corresponding view privileges are revoked from roles and users. After the view is re-created, necessary privileges must be regranted.

- A view can be replaced by redefining it with a CREATE VIEW statement that contains the OR REPLACE option. This option replaces the current definition of a view, but preserves the present security authorizations.

CREATE OR REPLACE VIEW Accounts_staff AS

SELECT Empno, Ename, Deptno FROM Emp WHERE Deptno = 30

WITH CHECK OPTION CONSTRAINT ica_Accounts_cnst;

Replacing a view has the following effects:

- Replacing a view replaces the view's definition in the data dictionary. All underlying objects referenced by the view are not affected.

- If previously defined but not included in the new view definition, then the constraint associated with the WITH CHECK OPTION for a view's definition is dropped.

- All views and PL/SQL program units dependent on a replaced view become invalid.

With some restrictions, rows can be inserted into, updated in, or deleted from a base table using a view. The following statement inserts a new row into the EMP table using the ACCOUNTS_STAFF view:

INSERT INTO Accounts_staff VALUES (199, 'Hemanth', 30);

Restrictions on DML operations for views use the following criteria in the order listed:

1. If a view is defined by a query that contains SET or DISTINCT operators, a GROUP BY clause, or a group function, then rows cannot be inserted into, updated in, or deleted from the base tables using the view.

2. If a view is defined with WITH CHECK OPTION, then a row cannot be inserted into, or updated in, the base table (using the view), if the view cannot select the row from the base table.

3. If a NOT NULL column that does not have a DEFAULT clause is omitted from the view, then a row cannot be inserted into the base table using the view.

4. If the view was created by using an expression, such as DECODE (deptno, 10, "SALES", ...), then rows cannot be inserted into or updated in the base table using the view.

The constraint created by WITH CHECK OPTION of the ACCOUNTS_STAFF view only allows rows that have a department number of 10 to be inserted into, or updated in, the EMP table. Alternatively, assume that the ACCOUNTS_STAFF view is defined by the following statement (that is, excluding the DEPTNO column):

CREATE VIEW Accounts_staff AS SELECT Empno, Ename FROM Emp

WHERE Deptno = 10 WITH CHECK OPTION CONSTRAINT ica_Accounts_cnst;

Considering this view definition, you can update the EMPNO or ENAME fields of existing records, but you cannot insert rows into the EMP table through the ACCOUNTS_STAFF view because the view does not let you alter the DEPTNO field. If you had defined a DEFAULT value of 10 on the DEPTNO field, then you could perform inserts.

If you don't want any DML operations to be performed on views, create them WITH READ ONLY option. Then no DML operations are allowed on views.

Modifying a Join View

Oracle allows you, with some restrictions, to modify views that involve joins. Consider the following simple view:

CREATE VIEW Emp_view AS SELECT Ename, Empno, deptno FROM Emp;

This view does not involve a join operation. If you issue the SQL statement:

UPDATE Emp_view SET Ename = 'king' WHERE Empno = 109;

then the EMP base table that underlies the view changes, and employee 109's name changes from 'sudasan' to 'king' in the EMP table.

However, if you create a view that involves a join operation, such as:

CREATE VIEW Emp_dept_view AS

  SELECT e.Empno, e.Ename, e.Deptno, e.Sal, d.Dname, d.Loc

    FROM Emp e, Dept d   /* JOIN operation */

    WHERE e.Deptno = d.Deptno   AND d.Loc IN ('HYD', 'BOM', 'DEL');

then there are restrictions on modifying either the EMP or the DEPT base table through this view.

A **modifiable join view** is a view that contains more than one table in the top-level FROM clause of the SELECT statement, and that does *not* contain any of the following:

- DISTINCT operator
- Aggregate functions: AVG, COUNT, GLB, MAX, MIN, STDDEV, SUM, or VARIANCE

- Set operations: UNION, UNION ALL, INTERSECT, MINUS
- GROUP BY or HAVING clauses
- START WITH or CONNECT BY clauses
- ROWNUM pseudocolumn

Any UPDATE, INSERT, or DELETE statement on a join view can modify *only one underlying base table*.

A view contains rows and columns, just like a real table. The fields in a view are fields from one or more real tables in the database.

You can add SQL functions, WHERE, and JOIN statements to a view and present the data as if the data were coming from one single table.

A view always shows up-to-date data, that is dynamic data. The database engine recreates the data, using the view's SQL statement, every time a user queries a view. A view is, in essence, a virtual table. It does not physically exist. Rather, it is created by a query joining one or more tables.

Updating a VIEW

You can update a VIEW without dropping it by using the following syntax:

CREATE OR REPLACE VIEW view_name AS SELECT columns FROM table WHERE predicates;

For example:

CREATE or REPLACE VIEW sup_orders AS SELECT suppliers.supplier_id, orders.quantity, orders.price FROM suppliers, orders WHERE suppliers.supplier_id = orders.supplier_id and suppliers.supplier_name = 'Microsoft';

SQL Dropping a View

You can delete a view with the DROP VIEW command.

SQL DROP VIEW Syntax for dropping a VIEW is:

DROP VIEW Accounts_staff;

DROP VIEW view_name

DROP VIEW sup_orders;

A view is created by joining one or more tables. When you update record(s) in a view, it updates the records in the underlying tables that make up the view. So, we can update the data in a view providing we have the proper privileges to the underlying tables.

Prerequisites

To create a view in your own schema, you must have the CREATE VIEW system privilege. To create a view in another user's schema, you must have the CREATE ANY VIEW system privilege.

To create a subview, you must have the UNDER ANY VIEW system privilege or the UNDER object privilege on the superview.

The owner of the schema containing the view must have the privileges necessary to either select, insert, update, or delete rows from all the tables or views on which the view is based. The owner must be granted these privileges directly, rather than through a role.

A view consists of a stored query accessible as a virtual table in a relational database.

Views can provide advantages over tables:

- Views can represent a subset of the data contained in a table
- Views can join and simplify multiple tables into a single virtual table
- Views can act as aggregated tables, where the database engine aggregates data (sum, average etc.) and presents the calculated results as part of the data
- Views can hide the complexity of data; for example a view could appear as Sales2000 or Sales2001, transparently partitioning the actual underlying table
- Views take very little space to store; the database contains only the definition of a view, not a copy of all the data it presents
- Depending on the SQL engine used, views can provide extra security
- Views can limit the degree of exposure of a table or tables to the outer world
- INSERT, UPDATE, and DELETE operations can be performed on updatable views.

SQL Data Types

The following is a list of general SQL data types that may not be supported by all relational databases.

Data Type	Syntax	Explanation (if applicable)
numeric	numeric(p,s)	Where *p* is a precision value; *s* is a scale value. For example, numeric(6,2) is a number that has 4 digits before the decimal and 2 digits after the decimal.
decimal	decimal(p,s)	Where *p* is a precision value; *s* is a scale value.
real	real	Single-precision floating point number
double precision	double precision	Double-precision floating point number
float	float(p)	Where *p* is a precision value.
character	char(x)	Where *x* is the number of characters to store. This data type is space padded to fill the number of characters specified.
character varying	varchar2(x)	Where *x* is the number of characters to store. This data type does NOT space pad.
bit	bit(x)	Where *x* is the number of bits to store.
bit varying	bit varying(x)	Where *x* is the number of bits to store. The length can vary up to x.
date	date	Stores year, month, and day values.
time	time	Stores the hour, minute, and second values.
timestamp	timestamp	Stores year, month, day, hour, minute, and second values.
time with time zone	time with time zone	Exactly the same as time, but also stores an offset from UTC of the time specified.
timestamp with time zone	timestamp with time zone	Exactly the same as timestamp, but also stores an offset from UTC of the time specified.
year-month interval		Contains a year value, a month value, or both.
day-time interval		Contains a day value, an hour value, a minute value, and/or a second value.

PL/SQL

PL/SQL (Procedural Language/Structured Query Language) is Oracle Corporation's procedural extension language for SQL and the Oracle relational database PL/SQL supports variables, conditions, loops and exceptions. Arrays are also supported,

PL/SQL Data Types

Every constant, variable, and parameter has a data type (also called a type) that determines its storage format, constraints, valid range of values, and operations that can be performed on it. PL/SQL provides many predefined data types and subtypes.

A subtype is a subset of another data type, which is called its base type. A subtype has the same valid operations as its base type, but only a subset of its valid values.

Table Categories of Predefined PL/SQL Data Types

Data Type Category	Data Description
Scalar	Single values with no internal components.
Composite	Data items that have internal components that can be accessed individually.
Reference	Pointers to other data items.
Large Object (LOB)	Pointers to large objects that are stored separately from other data items, such as text, graphic images, video clips, and sound waveforms.

Predefined PL/SQL Scalar Data Types and Subtypes

Scalar data types store single values with no internal components. Following table lists the predefined PL/SQL scalar data types and describes the data they store.

Categories of Predefined PL/SQL Scalar Data Types

Category	Data Description
Numeric	Numeric values, on which you can perform arithmetic operations.
Character	Alphanumeric values that represent single characters or strings of characters, which you can manipulate.
BOOLEAN	Logical values, on which you can perform logical operations.
Datetime	Dates and times, which you can manipulate.
Interval	Time intervals, which you can manipulate.

Predefined PL/SQL Numeric Data Types and Subtypes

Numeric data types let you store numeric data, represent quantities, and perform calculations. Following table lists the predefined PL/SQL numeric types and describes the data they store.

Table 3-3 Predefined PL/SQL Numeric Data Types

Data Type	Data Description
PLS_INTEGER or BINARY_INTEGER	Signed integer in range -2,147,483,648 through 2,147,483,647, represented in 32 bits
BINARY_FLOAT	Single-precision IEEE 754-format floating-point number
BINARY_DOUBLE	Double-precision IEEE 754-format floating-point number
NUMBER	Fixed-point or floating-point number with absolute value in range 1E-130 to (but not including) 1.0E126. A NUMBER variable can also represent 0.

9.7 Self Assessment Questions

9.7.1 Short Answer Questions

1. Define schema.

2. Define database schema.

3. Define database instance.

4. Define a view.

5. What are the advantages of views?

9.7.2 Essay Questions

1. Explain views with examples in detail.

2. What are SQL data types? Give examples.

3. What are PL/SQL data types? Give examples.

4. Explain SQL DDL commands in detail with examples.

CHAPTER 10

DATA MANIPULATION

Objectives

- ✓ To know about DML statements
- ✓ To understand INSERT statement
- ✓ To understand UPDATE statement
- ✓ To understand DELETE statement
- ✓ To understand SELECT statement
- ✓ To know about joins

Chapter Structure

10.1   Data Manipulation Language (DML) Statements

10.2   INSERT Statement

10.3   UPDATE Statement

10.4   DELETE Statement

10.5   SELECT Statement

10.6   JOINS

10.7   Query Languages

10.8   Graphical Query Language

10.9   Self Assessment Questions

10.1 Data Manipulation Language (DML) Statements or Commands

DML statements are used to manipulate data in tables.

Data manipulation language (DML) is the part of SQL that deals with inserting, updating, deleting and querying records in tables, views. DML statements access and manipulate data in existing schema objects. These statements do not implicitly commit the current transaction. The data manipulation language statements or commands are:

1. INSERT
2. UPDATE
3. DELETE
4. SELECT

The following types of actions may be performed using DML commands:

10.2 INSERT Statement

Insert command is used to add one or more records to a table. While inserting a record using the insert statement, the number of record values being entered should match the columns of the table. In case the number of items being entered are less than the number of columns, in that case the field names also need to be specified along with the insert statement. For example,

Consider a table named employees with the following fields: Emp_Id, FirstName, LastName, Height, Weight, The syntax to insert a record in this table will be:

INSERT INTO EMPLOYEES VALUES ('445','Cheruku','Sudharsan','6ft','85kg');

One example is given to insert a record into only selected columns INSERT INTO EMPLOYEES (Emp_Id, FirstName, Height) VALUES ('445','Raghu Rama Reddy','6ft');

Further, an insert statement can also be used in combination with select statement. What we can do is that the result of the select statement may be used as the values to be inserted in a table as

INSERT INTO EMPLOYEES SELECT * FROM STUDENT

WHERE FirstName IN ('Sudharsan', 'Sri Lakshmi','Hemanth','Ramya Shree'); You may even insert specific columns like below:

INSERT INTO EMPLOYEES (Emp_Id, FirstName) SELECT Emp_Id, FirstName FROM STUDENT WHERE FirstName NOT IN ('Anil', 'Venkat,'Cheruku','Yalamuri');

10.3 UPDATE statement

The update statement is used to change values that are already in a table. Update command is used to modify or edit the record or records of a table. It may be used to update a single row based on a condition, all rows, or a set of rows based on a condition.

It is used along with the **set** clause. Optionally, a **where** clause may be used to match conditions.

UPDATE TABLE EMPLOYEES

SET FIRSTNAME = 'Prasad' WHERE EMP_ID = '445'; Update the value of a column UPDATE TABLE EMPLOYEES SET AGE = AGE + 12;

Update multiple columns in one statement UPDATE TABLE EMP_SAL SET BONUS = BONUS + 10000, BASIC = BASIC + (0.2 * BONUS);

10.4 DELETE Statement

Delete command is used to remove one or more records from a table. All records may be removed in one delete statement or a set of records may be deleted based on a condition.

DELETE FROM EMPLOYEES WHERE FIRSTNAME = 'Cheruku';

Code below deletes records based on a condition

DELETE FROM STUDENT WHERE AGE < 18 ;

Delete may also be done based on the result of a sub query:

DELETE FROM STUDENT WHERE AGE IN

(SELECT AGE FROM STUDENT WHERE AGE < 18)

10.5 SELECT Statement

SELECT is considered to be part of DML even though it just retrieves data rather than modifying it. The SELECT statement is a limited form of DML statement in that it can only access data in the database. It cannot manipulate data in the database, although it can operate on the accessed data before returning the results of the query. This command is used to fetch a result set of records from a table, view or a group of tables, views by making use of SQL joins.

Retrieval of data using SELECT statement can be done by using different predicates along with it like – Where, group by, having, order by

To retrieve all records from the table EMP, the query is   SELECT * FROM EMP

To retrieve records from the table STUDENT so that age > 12 and below 16 the query is

SELECT * FROM STUDENT where age > 12 and age < 16;

To select records of students whose names begin with R, the query is

SELECT * FROM STUDENT where name like 'R%'

To select records of students whose names not begin with R, the query is

SELECT * FROM STUDENT where name not like 'R%'

The **Group By** statement in SQL is used for aggregation, which means that the result that is returned is based on grouping of results based on a column aggregation.

Select deptno, max(sal), min(sal), count(sal), avg(sal), sum(sal)

from emp

group by deptno

The **Having** statement in SQL makes sure that an SQL SELECT statement should only return rows where aggregate values match conditions that are stated.

Select deptno, max(sal), min(sal), count(sal), avg(sal), sum(sal)

from emp

group by deptno having avg(sal) > 2600

The **Order By** clause in SQL is used to set the order or sequence of the output in terms of being alphabetical, numerical, order of date. It may be accompanied by an 'asc' or 'desc' clause so as to specify whether the results are in ascending or descending order. The result of a select query that does not use asc or desc is in ascending order, by default.

Select empno, ename, sal, deptno from EMP order by sal;

Select empno, ename, sal, deptno from EMP order by sal asc;

Select empno, ename, sal, deptno from EMP order by sal desc;

Select empno, ename, sal, deptno from EMP order by deptno;

Select empno, ename, sal, deptno from EMP order by deptno asc;

Select empno, ename, sal, deptno from EMP order by deptno desc;

Select empno, ename, sal, deptno from EMP order by deptno, sal;

10.6 JOINS in SQL

SQL JOINS

SQL Joins are used to relate information in different tables. A Join condition is a part of the SQL query that retrieves rows from two or more tables. A SQL Join condition is used in the SQL WHERE Clause of select, update, delete statements.

The Syntax for joining two tables is:

SELECT col1, col2, col3... FROM table_name1, table_name2 WHERE table_name1.col2 = table_name2.col1;

If a SQL join condition is omitted or if it is invalid the join operation will result in a Cartesian product. The Cartesian product returns a number of rows equal to the product of all rows in all the tables being joined. For example, if the first table has 20 rows and the second table has 10 rows, the result will be 20 * 10, or 200 rows. This query takes a long time to execute.

The JOIN keyword is used in an SQL statement to query data from two or more tables, based on a relationship between certain columns in these tables. Tables in a database are often related to each other with keys.

SQL Joins can be classified into Equi join and Non Equi join.

10.6.1 SQL Equijoins or Inner Joins or Simple Joins

The inner join is also known as an equi-join. An inner join (sometimes called a simple join) is a join of two or more tables that returns only those rows that satisfy the join condition. An equijoin is a join with a join condition containing an equality operator. It is a simple SQL join condition which uses the equal sign as the comparison operator. An equijoin combines rows that have equivalent values for the specified columns.

An *inner join* is a join that selects only those records from both database tables that have matching values. Records with values in the joined field that do not appear in both of the database tables will be excluded from the query. One or more fields can serve as the join fields.

Two types of equi-joins are SQL Outer join and SQL Inner join.

For example: You can get the information about a customer who purchased a product and the quantity of product.

10.6.2 SQL Non-Equi Joins

A Non Equi Join is a SQL Join whose condition is established using all comparison operators except the equal (=) operator. Like >, >=, <, <=,

For example: If you want to find the names of students who are not studying Economics, the SQL query would be like

SELECT first_name, last_name, subject

FROM student_details WHERE subject != 'Economics'

10.6.3 SQL Inner Join

All the rows returned by the SQL query satisfy the SQL join condition specified.

For example: If you want to display the product information for each order the query will be as given below. Since you are retrieving the data from two tables, you need to identify the common column between these two tables, which is the product_id. The query for this type of SQL joins would be like,

SELECT order_id, product_name, unit_price, supplier_name, total_units FROM product, order_items WHERE order_items.product_id = product.product_id;

The columns must be referenced by the table name in the join condition, because product_id is a column in both the tables and needs a way to be identified. This avoids ambiguity in using the columns in the SQL SELECT statement.

We can also use aliases to reference the table name, then the above query would be like, SELECT o.order_id, p.product_name, p.unit_price, p.supplier_name, o.total_units FROM product p, order_items o WHERE o.product_id = p.product_id;

10.6.4 Cartesian Products

If two tables in a join query have no join condition, then Oracle database returns their Cartesian product. Oracle combines each row of one table with each row of the other. A Cartesian product always generates many rows and is rarely useful. For example, the Cartesian product of two tables, each with 100 rows, has 10,000 rows. Always include a join condition unless you specifically need a Cartesian product. If a query joins three or more tables and you do not specify a join condition for a specific pair, then the query optimizer may choose a join order that avoids producing an intermediate Cartesian product.

10.6.5 Self Joins

A Self Join is a type of SQL join which is used to join a table to itself. Same table appears twice in the FROM clause. Particularly when the table has a FOREIGN KEY that references its own PRIMARY KEY. It is necessary to ensure that the join statement defines an alias for both copies of the table to avoid column ambiguity. To perform a self join, Oracle database combines and returns rows of the table that satisfy the join condition. The below query is an example of a self join, SELECT a.sales_person_id, a.name, a.manager_id, b.sales_person_id, b.name FROM sales_person a, sales_person b WHERE a.manager_id = b.sales_person_id;

10.6.6 Outer Joins

This SQL join condition returns all rows from both tables which satisfy the join condition along with rows which do not satisfy the join condition from one of the tables. The SQL outer join operator in Oracle is (+) and is used on one side of the join condition only.

The syntax differs for different RDBMS implementation. Few of them represent the join conditions as "SQL left outer join", "SQL right outer join".

If you want to display all the product data along with order items data, with null values displayed for order items if a product has no order item, the SQL query for outer join would be as shown below:

SELECT   p.product_id,   p.product_name,   o.order_id,   o.total_units
FROM order_items o, product p WHERE o.product_id (+) = p.product_id;

If the (+) operator is used in the left side of the join condition it is equivalent to left outer join. If used on the right side of the join condition it is equivalent to right outer join.

An outer join extends the result of a simple join. An outer join returns all rows that satisfy the join condition and also returns some or all of those rows from one table for which no rows from the other satisfy the join condition.

- To write a query that performs an outer join of tables A and B and returns all rows from A (a left outer join), use the LEFT [OUTER] JOIN syntax in the FROM clause, or apply the outer join operator (+) to all columns of B in the join condition in the WHERE clause. For all rows in A that have no matching rows in B, Oracle database returns null for any select list expressions containing columns of B.

- To write a query that performs an outer join of tables A and B and returns all rows from B (a right outer join), use the RIGHT [OUTER] JOIN syntax in the FROM clause, or apply the outer join operator (+) to all columns of A in the join condition in the WHERE clause. For all rows in B that have no matching rows in A, Oracle returns null for any select list expressions containing columns of A.

- To write a query that performs an outer join and returns all rows from A and B, extended with nulls if they do not satisfy the join condition (a full outer join), use the FULL [OUTER] JOIN syntax in the FROM clause.

10.6.7 Natural join

A natural join is the most commonly used form of join operation. A natural join is the same as an equijoin except that it is performed over matching columns that have been defined with the same name, and one of the duplicate columns is eliminated.

10.7 Query Languages

SQL

SQL stands for structured query language. SQL is the standard database language for all relational database managements (RDBMSs).

Relational Algebra

Relational algebra is another formal query language based on a set of operators (select, project, Cartesian product) for manipulating relations.

Relational calculus

Relational calculus is a formal query language based on mathematical logic.

Very attractive feature of the relational data model is that it supports powerful query languages. A DBMS allows users to create, insert, modify, delete and query data through a data manipulation language (DML)

When several users access, modify, delete data in the same database concurrently, the DBMS must order their requests carefully in order to avoid conflicts. Without concurrent data access in the database degrades system performance. One main function of DBMS is to control concurrent access to the data stored in the database. A database is shared by a large number of database users.

10.8 Graphical Query Language

Text based queries often lead tend to be complex, and may result in non user friendly query structures. However, querying information systems using graphical means, even for complex queries have proven to be more efficient and effective as compared to text based queries. This is owing to the fact that graphical or visual systems make it easy way for better human-computer communication. Improved query systems are available using a Graphical or Visual Query Language. The system allows the users to construct query graphs by interacting with the ontology in a user friendly manner. The main purpose of the graphical query system is to enable efficient querying on ontologies even by novice users who do not have an in-depth knowledge of internal query structures. The system also supports graphical recursive queries and methods to interpret recursive programs from these graphical or visual query graphs.

PICASSO (PICture Aided Sophisticated Sketch Of database queries) is a graphics-based database query language designed for use with a universal relation database system. The primary objective of PICASSO is ease of use. Graphics are used to provide a simple method of expressing queries and to provide visual feedback to the user about the system's interpretation of the query. Inexperienced users can use the graphical feedback to aid them in formulating queries whereas experienced users can ignore the feedback. Inexperienced users can pose queries without knowing the details of underlying database schema and without learning the formal syntax of SQL-like query language.

This paper presents the syntax of PICASSO queries and compares PICASSO queries with similar queries in standard relational query languages. Comparisons are also made with System/U, a non-graphical universal relation system on which PICASSO is based. The hypergraph semantics of the universal relation are used as the foundation for PICASSO and their integration with a graphical workstation enhances the usability of database systems.

One of the main problems in the database area is to define query languages characterized by both high expressive power and ease of use. The system, called Query by Diagram * (QBD *), makes use of a conceptual data model, a query language on this model and a graphical user interface. The conceptual model is the Entity-Relationship Model; the query language, whose expressive power allows recursive queries, supports visual interaction. The main characteristics of the interface are the ease of use, and the availability of a rich set of primitives for schema selection and query formulation. Furthermore, we can compare the expressive power of QBD * and G + , which are the only languages allowing recursive queries to be expressed graphically

GRAQULA is a graphical language for querying and updating a database. One version of GRAQULA provides a user interface for the entity-relationship data model, and another version (with almost identical syntax) provides a user interface for the relational model. Each version is relationally complete, and each depicts relationships (or expected joins) graphically, GRAQULA provides logical operations (e.g. negation) on graphical objects; these operations have user-specified scopes, allow nesting, and can involve existential or universal quantification. Aggregates (e.g. average) also have user-specified scopes. Queries can invoke other queries, and users and queries can pass parameters to queries. The design reflects a specified set of goals, including expressive power, consistency, and limitation of required memorization.

SQL> INSERT INTO COURSE VALUES (10,'M.Tech',96452,'2 YEARS');

SQL> INSERT INTO COURSE VALUES (20,'B.Tech',76543,'4 YEARS');

SQL> INSERT INTO COURSE VALUES (30,'M.C.A',55443,'3 YEARS');

SQL> INSERT INTO COURSE VALUES (40,'B.Com',16500,'3 YEARS');

SQL> INSERT INTO COURSE VALUES (50,'M.Tech',96452,'2 years')

SQL> INSERT INTO COURSE VALUES (60,'B.Com',16500,'3 YEARS');

SQL> INSERT INTO COURSE VALUES (70,'B.Com',16500,'3 YEARS');

SQL> SELECT * FROM COURSE;

COURSE_ID	COURSE_NAME	FEE	DURATION
10	M.Tech	96452	2 YEARS
20	B.Tech	76543	4 YEARS
30	M.C.A	55443	3 YEARS
40	B.Com	16500	3 YEARS
50	M.Tech	96452	2 YEARS
60	B.Com	16500	3 YEARS
70	B.Com	16500	3 YEARS

7 rows selected.

SQL> INSERT INTO COURSE
VALUES(&COURSE_ID,'&COURSE_NAME',&FEE, '&DURATION');

SQL>INSERT INTO COURSE VALUES(&COURSE_ID,'&COURSE_NAME',&FEE, '&DURATION')

SQL> INSERT INTO COURSE
VALUES(&COURSE_ID,'&COURSE_NAME',&FEE, '&DURATION')

SQL> INSERT INTO COURSE
VALUES(&COURSE_ID,'&COURSE_NAME',&FEE, '&DURATION')

SQL>INSERT INTO COURSE VALUES(99,'M.C.A',32199, '3 YEARS')

SQL> COMMIT

SQL> SELECT * FROM COURSE;

COURSE_ID	COURSE_NAME	FEE	DURATION
10	M.Tech	96452	2 YEARS
20	B.Tech	76543	4 YEARS
30	M.C.A	55443	3 YEARS
40	B.Com	16500	3 YEARS
50	M.Tech	96452	2 YEARS
60	B.Com	16500	3 YEARS
70	B.Com	16500	3 YEARS
80	B.Tech	34500	4 YEARS
90	B.Tech	56000	4 YEARS
99	M.C.A	32199	3 YEARS

10 rows selected.

SQL> INSERT INTO STUDENT VALUES(1111,'RAMA','12-JAN-2001',10);

SQL> INSERT INTO STUDENT VALUES(2222,'BHEEMA','16-JUN-2002',10);

SQL> INSERT INTO STUDENT VALUES(3333,'DHARMA','29-DEC-2003',20);

SQL> INSERT INTO STUDENT VALUES

(&STUDENT_ID,'&STUDENT_NAME','&JOIN_DATE',&COURSE_ID);

Enter value for student_id: 4444

Enter value for student_name: ARJUNA

Enter value for join_date: 16-NOV-2004

Enter value for course_id: 30

Similarly you enter records for NAKULA, SAHADEVA, and ANJI

SQL> COMMIT;

SQL> SELECT * FROM STUDENT;

STUDENT_ID	STUDENT_NAME	JOIN_DATE	COURSE_ID
1111	RAMA	12-JAN-01	10
2222	BHEEMA	16-JUN-02	10
3333	DHARMA	29-DEC-03	20
4444	ARJUNA	16-NOV-04	30
5555	NAKULA	30-JUN-05	40
6666	SAHADEVA	25-OCT-07	30
7777	ANJI	20-MAR-08	20

7 rows selected.

```
SQL> SELECT  *  FROM  DEPT;
      DEPTNO  DNAME        LOC

      ----------  --------------   -------------
        10     FINANCE      NEW YORK
        20     RESEARCH     DALLAS
        30     SALES        CHICAGO
        40     OPERATIONS   BOSTON
SQL> SELECT * FROM  EMP;
```

EMPNO	ENAME	JOB	MGR	HIREDATE	SAL	COMM	DEPTNO
7369	SMITH	CLERK	7902	17-DEC-80	800		20
7499	ALLEN	SALESMAN	7698	20-FEB-81	1600	300	30
7521	WARD	SALESMAN	7698	22-FEB-81	1250	500	30
7566	JONES	MANAGER	7839	02-APR-81	2975		20
7654	MARTIN	SALESMAN	7698	28-SEP-81	1250	1400	30
7698	BLAKE	MANAGER	7839	01-MAY-81	2850		30
7782	CLARK	MANAGER	7839	09-JUN-81	2450		10
7788	SCOTT	ANALYST	7566	19-APR-87	3000		20
7839	KING	PRESIDENT		17-NOV-81	5000		10
7844	TURNER	SALESMAN	7698	08-SEP-81	1500	0	30
7876	ADAMS	CLERK	7788	23-MAY-87	1100		20
7900	JAMES	CLERK	7698	03-DEC-81	950		30
7902	FORD	ANALYST	7566	03-DEC-81	3000		20
7934	MILLER	CLERK	7782	23-JAN-82	1300		10

14 rows selected.

1) select * from dept;

2) select * from emp;

3) select sal from emp;

4) select distinct sal from emp;

5) select all job from emp;

6) select distinct job from emp;

7) select * from emp where deptno = 10;

8) select * from emp where deptno = 10 and sal < 2000;

9) select * from emp where deptno = 30 and sal > 1000 and empno > 2000;

10) select * from emp where deptno = 30 and sal > 1000 and empno > 2000 and job = 'SALESMAN';

11) select * from emp where deptno = 20 or sal > 3000;

12) select sal, sal*10, sal+100 from emp;

13) select * from emp where mgr is null;

14) select * from emp where comm is null;

15) select * from emp where comm is not null;

16) select deptno,sal, nvl(comm, 0) from emp;

17) select * from emp where sal between 2000 and 3000;

18) select * from emp where sal not between 2000 and 3000;

19) select * from emp where sal >= 2000 and sal <= 3000;

20) select * from emp where length(ename) = 4;

21) select empno, ename, job from emp;

22) select * from emp where job = 'SALESMAN' and sal > 1000 and deptno = 30
            and empno > 1234

23) select * from emp order by sal;

24) select * from emp order by sal desc;

25) select * from emp order by deptno, sal;

26) select deptno, sal from emp;

27) select deptno, sal from emp order by deptno;

28) select deptno, sal from emp order by deptno, sal;

29) select * from emp where ename like 'S%';

30) select * from emp where ename not like 'S%';

31) select * from emp where ename like '___E_';

32) select * from emp where ename not like '___E_';

33) select * from emp where ename like '%E%';

34) select * from emp where ename like '%AM%';

35) select * from emp where job like '%MAN%';

36) select * from emp where ename like 'A%';

37) select * from emp where deptno in (30,40);

38) select * from emp where deptno not in (30,40,50);

39) select * from emp where deptno > any (20,30,40,50);

40) select * from emp where deptno > any (10,20,30,40,50);

41) select * from emp where deptno >= any (30,40,50);

42) select * from emp where deptno >= some (30,40,50);

43) select * from emp where deptno <= some (20,30,40);

44) select * from emp where deptno <= some (10,20);

45) select * from emp where deptno < all (20,30,40,50);

46) select * from emp where deptno > all (10,20);

47) select * from emp where deptno >= all (10,20);

48) select * from emp where sal < all (1000,2000,3000);

49) select * from emp where sal > all (1000,2000,3000) and deptno >= 10;

50) select job from emp where deptno=10 union all select job from emp where deptno=20;

51) select job from emp where deptno = 10 union select job from emp where deptno = 20;

52) select job from emp where deptno = 10 intersect select job from emp where deptno = 20;

53) select job from emp where deptno = 10 minus select job from emp where deptno = 20;

54) select deptno, job from emp where sal > 1000 union select deptno, job from emp where sal > 2000;

55) select deptno, job from emp where sal > 1000 intersect select deptno, job from emp where sal > 2000;

56) select deptno, job from emp where sal > 1000 minus select deptno, job from emp where sal > 2000;

57) select * from emp where deptno in (select deptno from dept);

58) select * from emp where deptno in (select deptno from dept where dname = 'SALES');

59) select * from emp where deptno < (select deptno from dept where dname = 'SALES');

60) select * from emp where deptno < any (select deptno from dept);

61) select * from emp where deptno <= any (select deptno from dept);

62) select * from emp where deptno < all (select deptno from dept);

63) select * from emp where deptno <= all (select deptno from dept);

64) select * from emp where deptno >= some (select deptno from dept);

65) select * from emp where exists (select deptno from dept where deptno > 20);

66) select * from emp where exists (select deptno from dept where deptno > 40);

67) select * from emp where not exists (select deptno from dept where deptno > 40);

68) select dept.deptno, dname, loc, emp.empno, ename, job from dept, emp;

69) select dept.deptno, dname, loc, emp.empno, ename, job from dept, emp where dept.deptno = emp.deptno;

70) select dept.deptno, dname, loc, emp.empno, ename, job from dept, emp where dept.deptno != emp.deptno;

71) select dept.deptno, dname, loc, emp.deptno, emp.empno, ename, job from dept, emp where dept.deptno > emp.deptno;

72) select a.deptno, b.deptno,job,sal from dept a, emp b;

73) select a.deptno, b.deptno,job,sal from dept a, emp b where a.deptno = b.deptno;

74) select a.deptno, b.deptno,job,sal from dept a, emp b where a.deptno = b.deptno(+);

75) select a.deptno, b.deptno,job,sal from dept a, emp b where a.deptno(+) = b.deptno

76) select * from emp a where a.sal >all (select b.sal from emp b where a.sal > b.sal);

77) select * from emp a where a.sal >all (select b.sal from emp b where a.sal < b.sal);

78) select * from emp a where &n = (select count(b.sal) from emp b where a.sal <= b.sal); //to find n^{th} maximum salary from the table EMP;

79) select * from emp a where &n = (select count(b.sal) from emp b where a.sal >= b.sal); //to find n^{th} maximum salary from the table EMP;

80) select * from emp where substr(hiredate,4,3) = 'APR'; // to find all employees who joined in APRIL month

81) select * from emp where substr(hiredate,4,3) != 'APR'; // to find all employees who are not joined in APRIL month

82) select * from emp where substr(hiredate,4,3) = 'APR' or substr(hiredate,4,3) = 'DEC'; // to find employees who joined other than APRIL or DECEMBER

83) select   a.empno, a.ename,a.job, a.sal, a.comm, a.deptno from emp a, emp b where substr(to_char(a.empno),3,2) = substr(b.hiredate,8,2); // to find all employees whose last two digits in their empno is same as year in the joining date of any employee

84) select   a.empno, a.ename,a.job, a.sal, a.comm, a.deptno from emp a, emp b where substr(to_char(a.empno),1,2) = substr(b.sal,3,2); // to find all employees whose first two digits in their empno is same as the last two digits of the salary of any employee

85)   select * from emp where exists (select * from dept);

86)   Select * from emp where not exists(select * from dept);

87)   Select dept.deptno, emp.deptno from dept, emp;

88)   Select dept.deptno. empno,sal from dept,emp;

SQL> select max(sal), min(sal), count(sal), sum(sal), avg(sal) from emp;

MAX(SAL)	MIN(SAL)	COUNT(SAL)	SUM(SAL)	AVG(SAL)
5000	800	14	29025	2073.21429

SQL> select count(sal), count(comm) from emp;

COUNT(SAL)	COUNT(COMM)
14	4

SQL> select deptno, max(sal),min(sal), sum(sal) from emp group by deptno;

DEPTNO	MAX(SAL)	MIN(SAL)	SUM(SAL)
30	2850	950	9400
20	3000	800	10875
10	5000	1300	8750

SQL> select deptno, max(sal),min(sal), sum(sal) from emp group by deptno order by deptno;

DEPTNO	MAX(SAL)	MIN(SAL)	SUM(SAL)
10	5000	1300	8750
20	3000	800	10875
30	2850	950	9400

SQL> select deptno, max(sal),min(sal), sum(sal) from emp group by deptno

having sum(sal) >= 3000 order by deptno;

DEPTNO	MAX(SAL)	MIN(SAL)	SUM(SAL)
10	5000	1300	8750
20	3000	800	10875
30	2850	950	9400

SQL> select deptno, max(sal),min(sal), sum(sal) from emp group by deptno

having max(sal) > 3000 order by deptno

DEPTNO	MAX(SAL)	MIN(SAL)	SUM(SAL)
10	5000	1300	8750

10.9 Self Assessment Questions

10.1 Short Answer Questions

1. What are DML statements?

2. What is SQL?

3. What are different types of query languages?

4. What is a join?

5. What is an outer join?

6. What is a query?

7. What is a sub query?

8. What is a correlated query?

9. What is a graphical query?

10.2 Essay Questions

1. What are data manipulation (DML) commands? Explain in detail with examples.

2. What are joins? Explain with examples.

3. What are different types of queries? Explain with examples in detail.

4. What are aggregate operators? Explain with examples.

5. Explain group by, having, order by clauses with examples.

References

1. Mark L. Gillenson, Frank Miller Wiley Pathways Introduction to Database Management Project Manual.

2. Mark L. Gillenson Fundamentals of Database Management Systems, 2nd Edition.

3. **Sumathi**, S., **Esakkirajan**, S. Fundamentals of Relational Database Management Systems

4. E.F. Codd (1970). "A relational model of data for large shared data banks". In: *Communications of the ACM archive*. Vol 13. Issue 6(June 1970). pp.377-387.

5. **Jump up** *Introducing databases* by Stephen Chu, in Conrick, M. (2006) *Health informatics: transforming healthcare with technology*, Thomson, ISBN 0-17-012731-1, p. 69.

6. **Jump up** Date, C. J. (June 1, 1999). "When's an extension not an extension?". *Intelligent Enterprise* **2** (8).

7. **Jump up** Zhuge, H. (2008). *The Web Resource Space Model*. Web Information Systems Engineering and Internet Technologies Book Series **4**. Springer. ISBN 978-0-387-72771-4.

8. The DBAZine (www.dbazine.com), the Intelligent Enterprise magazine (www. iemagazine.com), and the Advisor.com (www.advisor.com) websites provide detailed technical information about commercial DBMSs, database design, and database application development. To learn more about the role of database specialists and information resource management, you should consult Mullin (2002).

9. Jeffrey Ullman 1997: *First course in database systems*, Prentice-Hall Inc., Simon & Schuster, Page 1, ISBN 0-13-861337-0.

10. Tsitchizris, D. C. and F. H. Lochovsky (1982). *Data Models.* Englewood-Cliffs, Prentice-Hall.

11. Beynon-Davies P. (2004). *Database Systems* 3rd Edition. Palgrave, Basingstoke, UK. ISBN 1-4039-1601-2

12. Raul F. Chong, Michael Dang, Dwaine R. Snow, Xiaomei Wang (3 July 2008). "Introduction to DB2". Retrieved 17 March 2013.. This article quotes a development time of 5 years involving 750 people for DB2 release 9 alone

13. C. W. Bachmann (November 1973), "The Programmer as Navigator", *CACM* (Turing Award Lecture 1973)

14. "database, n". *OED Online*. Oxford University Press. June 2013. Retrieved July 12, 2013.

15. Codd, E.F. (1970)."A Relational Model of Data for Large Shared Data Banks". In: *Communications of the ACM* 13 (6): 377–387.

16. William Hershey and Carol Easthope, "A set theoretic data structure and retrieval language", Spring Joint Computer Conference, May 1972 in *ACM SIGIR Forum*, Volume 7, Issue 4 (December 1972), pp. 45-55, DOI=10.1145/1095495.1095500

17. Ken North, "Sets, Data Models and Data Independence", *Dr. Dobb's*, 10 March 2010

18. *Description of a set-theoretic data structure*, D. L. Childs, 1968, Technical Report 3 of the CONCOMP (Research in Conversational Use of Computers) Project, University of Michigan, Ann Arbor, Michigan, USA

19. *Feasibility of a Set-Theoretic Data Structure : A General Structure Based on a Reconstituted Definition of Relation*, D. L. Childs, 1968, Technical Report 6 of the CONCOMP (Research in Conversational Use of Computers) Project, University of Michigan, Ann Arbor, Michigan, USA

20. *MICRO Information Management System (Version 5.0) Reference Manual*, M.A. Kahn, D.L. Rumelhart, and B.L. Bronson, October 1977, Institute of Labor and Industrial Relations (ILIR), University of Michigan and Wayne State University

21. Interview with Wayne Ratliff. The FoxPro History. Retrieved on 2013-07-12.

22. Development of an object-oriented DBMS; Portland, Oregon, United States; Pages: 472 – 482; 1986; ISBN 0-89791-204-7

23. "DB-Engines Ranking". January 2013. Retrieved 22 January 2013.

24. "TeleCommunication Systems Signs up as a Reseller of TimesTen; Mobile Operators and Carriers Gain Real-Time Platform for Location-Based Services". *Business Wire*. 2002-06-24.

25. Graves, Steve. "COTS Databases For Embedded Systems", *Embedded Computing Design* magazine, January 2007. Retrieved on August 13, 2008.

26. Argumentation in Artificial Intelligence by Iyad Rahwan, Guillermo R. Simari

27. "OWL DL Semantics". Retrieved 10 December 2010.

28. itl.nist.gov (1993) *Integration Definition for Information Modeling (IDEFIX)*. 21 December 1993. Date 1990, pp. 31–32

29. Chapple, Mike. "SQL Fundamentals". *Databases*. About.com. Retrieved 2009-01-28.

30. "Structured Query Language (SQL)". International Business Machines. October 27, 2006. Retrieved 2007-06-10.

31. Wagner, Michael (2010), "1. Auflage", *SQL/XML:2006 - Evaluierung der Standardkonformität ausgewählter Datenbanksysteme*, Diplomica Verlag, ISBN 3-8366-9609-6

www.ingramcontent.com/pod-product-compliance
Lightning Source LLC
Chambersburg PA
CBHW080417060326
40689CB00019B/4279